# Castle Rackrent by Maria Edgeworth

Maria Edgeworth was born at Black Bourton, Oxfordshire on January 1st 1768. Her early years were with her mother's family in England. Sadly, her mother died when Maria was five.

Maria was educated at Mrs Lattafière's school in Derby in 1775. There she studied dancing, French and other subjects. Maria transferred to Mrs Devis's school in Upper Wimpole Street, London. Her father began to focus more attention on Maria in 1781 when she nearly lost her sight to an eye infection.

She returned home to Ireland at 14 and took charge of her younger siblings. She herself was home-tutored by her father in Irish economics and politics, science, literature and law. Despite her youth literature was in her blood. Maria also became her father's assistant in managing the family's large Edgeworthstown estate.

Maria first published 1795 with 'Letters for Literary Ladies'. That same year 'An Essay on the Noble Science of Self-Justification', written for a female audience, advised women on how to obtain better rights in general and specifically from their husbands.

'Practical Education' (1798) is a progressive work on education. Maria's ambition was to create an independent thinker who understands the consequences of his or her actions.

Her first novel, 'Castle Rackrent' was published anonymously in 1800 without her father's knowledge. It was an immediate success and firmly established Maria's appeal to the public.

Her father married four times and the last of these to Frances, a year younger and a confidante of Maria, who pushed them to travel more widely: London, Britain and Europe were all now visited.

The second series of 'Tales of Fashionable Life' (1812) did so well that she was now the most commercially successful novelist of her age.

She particularly worked hard to improve the living standards of the poor in Edgeworthstown and to provide schools for the local children of all and any denomination.

After a visit to see her relations Maria had severe chest pains and died suddenly of a heart attack in Edgeworthstown on 22nd May 1849. She was 81.

## Index of Contents

## INTRODUCTION

I

The story of the Edgeworth Family, if it were properly told, should be as long as the ARABIAN NIGHTS themselves; the thousand and one cheerful intelligent members of the circle, the amusing friends and relations, the charming surroundings, the cheerful hospitable home, all go to make up an almost unique history of a county family of great parts and no little character. The Edgeworths were people of good means and position, and their rental, we are told, amounted to nearly L3000 a year. At one time there was some talk of a peerage for Mr. Edgeworth, but he was considered too independent for a peerage.

The family tradition seems to have been unconventional and spirited always. There are records still extant in the present Mr. Edgeworth's possession,—papers of most wonderful vitality for parchment,— where you may read passionate remonstrances and adjurations from great-grandfathers to great-great-grandfathers, and where great-great-grandmothers rush into the discussion with vehement spelling and remonstrance, and make matters no better by their interference. I never read more passionately eloquent letters and appeals. There are also records of a pleasanter nature; merrymakings, and festive preparations, and 12s. 6d. for a pair of silk stockings for Miss Margaret Edgeworth to dance in, carefully entered into the family budget. All the people whose portraits are hanging up, beruffled, dignified, calm, and periwigged, on the old walls of Edgeworthstown certainly had extraordinarily strong impressions, and gave eloquent expression to them. I don't think people could feel quite so strongly now about their own affairs as they did then; there are so many printed emotions, so many public events, that private details cannot seem quite as important. Edgeworths of those days were farther away from the world than they are now, dwelling in the plains of Longford, which as yet were not crossed by iron rails. The family seems to have made little of distances, and to have ridden and posted to and fro from Dublin to Edgeworthstown in storm and sunshine.

II

When Messrs. Macmillan asked me to write a preface to this new edition of Miss Edgeworth's stories I thought I should like to see the place where she had lived so long and where she had written so much, and so it happened that being in Ireland early this year, my daughter and I found ourselves driving up to Broadstone Station one morning in time for the early train to Edgeworthstown. As we got out of our cab we asked the driver what the fare should be. 'Sure the fare is half a crown,' said he, 'and if you wish to give me more, I could keep it for myself!'

The train was starting and we bought our papers to beguile the road. 'Will you have a Home Rule paper or one of them others?' said the newsboy, with such a droll emphasis that we couldn't help laughing. 'Give me one of each,' said I; then he laughed, as no English newsboy would have done. . . . We went along in the car with a sad couple of people out of a hospital, compatriots of our own, who had been settled ten years in Ireland, and were longing to be away. The poor things were past consolation, dull, despairing, ingrained English, sick and suffering and yearning for Brixton, just as other aliens long for their native hills and moors. We travelled along together all that spring morning by the blossoming hedges, and triumphal arches of flowering May; the hills were very far away, but the lovely lights and scents were all about and made our journey charming. Maynooth was a fragrant vision as we flew past, of vast gardens wall-enclosed, of stately buildings. The whole line of railway was sweet with the May flowers, and with the pungent and refreshing scent of the turf-bogs. The air was so clear and so limpid that we could see for miles, and short-sighted eyes needed no glasses to admire with. Here and there a turf cabin, now and then a lake placidly reflecting the sky. The country seemed given over to silence, the light sped unheeded across the delicate browns and greens of the bog-fields; or lay on the sweet wonderful green of the meadows. One dazzling field we saw full of dancing circles of little fairy pigs with curly tails. Everything was homelike but NOT England, there was something of France, something of Italy in the sky; in the fanciful tints upon the land and sea, in the vastness of the picture, in the happy sadness and calm content which is so difficult to describe or to account for. Finally we reached our journey's end. It gave one a real emotion to see EDGEWORTHSTOWN written up on the board before us, and to realise that we were following in the steps of those giants who had passed before us. The master of Edgeworthstown kindly met us and drove us to his home through the outlying village, shaded with its sycamores, underneath which pretty cows were browsing the grass. We passed the Roman Catholic Church, the great iron crucifix standing in the churchyard. Then the horses turned in at the gate of the park, and there rose the old home, so exactly like what one expected it, that I felt as if I had been there before in some other phase of existence.

It is certainly a tradition in the family to welcome travellers! I thought of the various memoirs I had read, of the travellers arriving from the North and the South and the West; of Scott and Lockhart, of Pictet, of the Ticknors, of the many visitants who had come up in turn; whether it is the year 14, or the year 94, the hospitable doors open kindly to admit them. There were the French windows reaching to the ground, through which Maria used to pass on her way to gather her roses; there was the porch where Walter Scott had stood; there grew the quaint old-fashioned bushes with the great pink peonies in flower, by those railings which still divide the park from the meadows beyond; there spread the branches of the century-old trees. Only last winter they told us the storms came and swept away a grove of Beeches that were known in all the country round, but how much of shade, of flower, still remain! The noble Hawthorn of stately growth, the pine-trees (there should be NAMES for trees, as there are for rocks or ancient strongholds). Mr. Edgeworth showed us the oak from Jerusalem, the grove of cypress and sycamore where the beautiful depths of ground ivy are floating upon the DEBRIS, and soften the gnarled roots, while they flood the rising banks with green.

Mr. and Mrs. Edgeworth brought us into the house. The ways go upstairs and downstairs, by winding passages and side gates; a pretty domed staircase starts from the central hall, where stands that old clock-case which Maria wound up when she was over eighty years old. To the right and to the left along the passages were rooms opening from one into another. I could imagine Sir Walter's kind eyes looking upon the scene, and Wordsworth coming down the stairs, and their friendly entertainer making all happy, and all welcome in turn; and their hostess, the widowed Mrs. Edgeworth, responding and sympathising with each. We saw the corner by the fire where Maria wrote; we saw her table with its pretty curves standing in its place in the deep casements. Miss Edgeworth's own room is a tiny little room above looking out on the back garden. This little closet opens from a larger one, and then by a narrow flight of stairs leads to a suite of ground-floor chambers, following one from another, lined with bookcases and looking on the gardens. What a strange fellow-feeling with the past it gave one to stand staring at the old books, with their paper backs and old-fashioned covers, at the gray boards, which were the liveries of literature in those early days; at the first editions, with their inscriptions in the author's handwriting, or in Maria's pretty caligraphy. There was the PIRATE in its original volumes, and Mackintosh's MEMOIRS, and Mrs. Barbauld's ESSAYS, and Descartes's ESSAYS, that Arthur Hallam liked to read; Hallam's CONSTITUTIONAL HISTORY, and Rogers's POEMS, were there all inscribed and dedicated. Not less interesting were the piles of Magazines that had been sent from America. I never knew before how many Magazines existed even those early days; we took some down at hazard and read names, dates, and initials. . . . Storied urn and monumental bust do not bring back the past as do the books which belong to it. Storied urns are in churches and stone niches, far removed from the lives of which they speak; books seem a part of our daily life, and are like the sound of a voice just outside the door. Here they were, as they had been read by her, stored away by her hands, and still safely preserved, bringing back the past with, as it were, a cheerful encouraging greeting to the present. Other relics there are of course, but, as I say, none which touch one so vividly. There is her silver ink-stand, the little table her father left her on which she wrote (it had belonged to his mother before him). There is also a curious trophy—a table which was sent to her from Edinburgh, ornamented by promiscuous views of Italy, curiously inappropriate to her genius; but not so the inscription, which is quoted from Sir Walter Scott's Preface to his Collected Edition, and which may as well be quoted here: 'WITHOUT BEING SO PRESUMPTUOUS AS TO HOPE TO EMULATE THE RICH HUMOUR, THE PATHETIC TENDERNESS, AND ADMIRABLE TRUTH WHICH PERVADE THE WORKS OF MY ACCOMPLISHED FRIEND,' Sir Walter wrote, I FELT THAT SOMETHING MIGHT BE ATTEMPTED FOR MY OWN COUNTRY OF THE SAME KIND AS THAT WHICH MISS EDGEWORTH SO FORTUNATELY ACHIEVED FOR IRELAND.'

In the MEMOIRS of Miss Edgeworth there is a pretty account of her sudden burst of feeling when this passage so unexpected, and so deeply felt by her, was read out by one of her sisters, at a time when Maria lay weak and recovering from illness in Edgeworthstown.

Our host took us that day, among other pleasant things, for a marvellous and delightful flight on a jaunting car, to see something of the country. We sped through storms and sunshine, by open moors and fields, and then by villages and little churches, by farms where the pigs were standing at the doors to be fed, by pretty trim cottages. The lights came and went; as the mist lifted we could see the exquisite colours, the green, the dazzling sweet lights on the meadows, playing upon the meadow-sweet and elder bushes; at last we came to the lovely glades of Carriglass. It seemed to me that we had reached an enchanted forest amid this green sweet tangle of ivy, of flowering summer trees, of immemorial oaks and sycamores.

A squirrel was darting up the branches of a beautiful spreading beech-tree, a whole army of rabbits were flashing with silver tails into the brushwood; swallows, blackbirds, peacock-butterflies, dragonflies on the wing, a mighty sylvan life was roaming in this lovely orderly wilderness.

The great Irish kitchen garden, belonging to the house, with its seven miles of wall, was also not unlike a part of a fairy tale. Its owner, Mr. Lefroy, told me that Miss Edgeworth had been constantly there. She was a great friend of Judge Lefroy. As a boy he remembered her driving up to the house and running up through the great drawing-room doors to greet the Judge.

Miss Edgeworth certainly lived in a fair surrounding, and, with Sophia Western, must have gone along the way of life heralded by sweetest things, by the song of birds, by the gold radiance of the buttercups, by the varied shadows of those beautiful trees under which the cows gently tread the grass. English does not seem exactly the language in which to write of Ireland, with its sylvan wonders of natural beauty. Madame de Sevigne's descriptions of her woods came to my mind. It is not a place which delights one by its actual sensual beauty, as Italy does; it is not as in England, where a thousand associations link one to every scene and aspect—Ireland seems to me to contain some unique and most impersonal charm, which is quite unwritable.

All that evening we sat talking with our hosts round the fire (for it was cold enough for a fire), and I remembered that in Miss Edgeworth's MEMOIRS it was described how the snow lay upon the ground and upon the land, when the family came home in June to take possession of Edgeworthstown.

As I put out my candle in the spacious guest-chamber I wondered which of its past inhabitants I should wish to see standing in the middle of the room. I must confess that the thought of the beautiful Honora filled me with alarm, and if Miss Seward had walked in in her pearls and satin robe I should have fled for my life. As I lay there experimentalising upon my own emotions I found that after all, natural simple people do not frighten one whether dead or alive. The thought of them is ever welcome; it is the artificial people who are sometimes one thing, sometimes another, and who form themselves on the weaknesses and fancies of those among whom they live, who are really terrifying.

The shadow of the bird's wing flitted across the window of my bedroom, and the sun was shining next morning when I awoke. I could see the cows, foot deep in the grass under the hawthorns. After breakfast we went out into the grounds and through an arched doorway into the kitchen garden. It might have been some corner of Italy or the South of France; the square tower of the granary rose high against the blue, the gray walls were hung with messy fruit trees, pigeons were darting and flapping their wings, gardeners were at work, the very vegetables were growing luxuriant and romantic and edged by thick borders of violet pansy; crossing the courtyard, we came into the village street, also orderly and white-washed. The soft limpid air made all things into pictures, into Turners, into Titians. A Murillo-like boy, with dark eyes, was leaning against a wall, with his shadow, watching us go by; strange old women, with draperies round their heads, were coming out of their houses. We passed the Post-Office, the village shops, with their names, the Monaghans and Gerahtys, such as we find again in Miss Edgeworth's novels. We heard the local politics discussed over the counter with a certain aptness and directness which struck me very much. We passed the boarding-house, which was not without its history—a long low building erected by Mr. and Miss Edgeworth for a school, where the Sandfords and Mertons of those days were to be brought up together: a sort of foreshadowing of the High Schools of the present. Mr. Edgeworth was, as we know, the very spirit of progress, though his experiment did not answer at the time. At the end of the village street, where two roads divide, we noticed a gap in the decent roadway—a pile of ruins in a garden. A tumble-down cottage, and beyond the cottage, a falling shed, on the thatched roof of which a hen was clucking and scraping. These cottages Mr. Edgeworth had, after long difficulty, bought up and condemned as unfit for human habitation. The plans had been considered, the orders given to build new cottages in their place, which were to be let to the old tenants at the old rent, but the last remaining inhabitant absolutely refused to leave; we saw an old woman in a hood slowly crossing the road, and carrying a pail for water; no threats or inducements would move her, not even the sight of a neat little house, white-washed and painted, and all ready for her to step into. Her present rent was 10d. a week, Mr. Edgeworth told me, and she had been letting the tumble-down shed to a large family for 1s. 4d. This sub-let was forcibly put an end to, but the landlady still stops there, and there she will stay until the roof tumbles down upon her head. The old creature passed on through the sunshine, a decrepit, picturesque figure carrying her pail to the stream, defying all the laws of progress and political economy and civilisation in her feebleness and determination.

Most of the women came to their doors to see us go by. They all looked as old as the hills—some dropt curtseys, others threw up their arms in benediction. From a cottage farther up the road issued a strange, shy old creature, looking like a bundle of hay, walking on bare legs. She came up with a pinch of snuff, and a shake of the hand; she was of the family of the man who had once saved Edgeworthstown from being destroyed by the rebels. 'Sure it was not her father,' said old Peggy,' it was her grandfather did it!'

So she explained, but it was hard to believe that such an old, old creature had ever had a grandfather in the memory of man.

The glebe lands lie beyond the village. They reach as far as the church on its high plateau, from which you can see the Wicklow Hills on a fine day, and the lovely shifting of the lights of the landscape. The remains of the great pew of the Edgeworth family, with its carved canopy of wood, is still a feature in the bare church from which so much has been swept away. The names of the fathers are written on the chancel walls, and a few medallions of daughters and sisters also. In the churchyard, among green elder bushes and tall upspringing grasses, is the square monument erected to Mr. Edgeworth and his family; and as we stood there the quiet place was crossed and recrossed by swallows with their beating crescent wings.

III

Whatever one may think of Mr. Edgeworth's literary manipulations and of his influence upon his daughter's writings, one cannot but respect the sincere and cordial understanding which bound these two people together, and realise the added interest in life, in its machinery and evolutions, which Maria owed to her father's active intelligence. Her own gift, I think, must have been one for perceiving through the minds of others, and for realising the value of what they in turn reflected; one is struck again and again by the odd mixture of intuition, and of absolute matter of fact which one finds in her writings.

It is difficult to realise, when one reads the memoirs of human beings who loved and hated, and laughed and scolded, and wanted things and did without them, very much as we do ourselves, that though they thought as we do and felt as we do (only, as I have said, with greater vehemence), they didn't LOOK like us at all; and Mr. Edgeworth, the father of Maria Edgeworth, the 'gay gallant,' the impetuous, ingenious, energetic gentleman, sat writing with powdered hair and a queue, with tights and buckles, bolt upright in a stiff chair, while his family, also bequeued and becurled and bekerchiefed, were gathered round him in a group, composedly attentive to his explanations, as he points to the roll upon the table, or reads from his many MSS. and notebooks, for their edification.

To have four wives and twenty-two children, to have invented so many machines, engines, and curricles, steeples and telegraph posts, is more than commonly falls to the lot of one ordinary man, but such we know was Mr. Edgeworth's history told by his own lips.

I received by chance an old newspaper the other day, dated the 23rd July 1779. It is called the LONDON PACKET, and its news, told with long s's and pretty curly italics, thrills one even now as one looks over the four short pages. The leading article is entitled 'Striking Instance of the PERFIDY of France.' It is true the grievance goes back to Louis XIV., but the leader is written with plenty of spirit and present indignation. Then comes news from America and the lists of New Councillors elected:

'Artemus Ward, Francis Dana, Oliver Prescott, Samuel Baker, while a very suitable sermon on the occasion is preached by the Rev. Mr. Stillman of Boston.' How familiar the names all sound! Then the thanks of the Members of Congress are given to 'General Lee, Colonel Moultrie, and the officers and soldiers under their command who on the 28th of June last Repulsed with so much Valour the attack that was made that day on the State of South Carolina by the fleet and army of his Britannic Majesty.'

There is an irresistible spirit of old-world pigtail decorum and dash about it all. We read of our 'grand fleet' waiting at Corunna for the Spanish; of 80,000 men on the coast of Brittany supposed to be ready for an invasion of England; of the Prince of Conde playing at cards, with Northumberland House itself for stakes (Northumberland House which he is INTENDING to take). We read the list of Lottery Prizes, of the L1000 and L500 tickets; of the pressing want of seamen for His Majesty's Navy, and how the gentlemen of Ireland are subscribers to a bounty fund. Then comes the narrative of James Caton of Bristol, who writes to complain that while transacting his business on the Bristol Exchange he is violently seized by a pressgang, with oaths and imprecations. Mr. Farr, attempting to speak to him, is told by the Lieutenant that if he does not keep off he will be shot with a pistol. Mr. Caton is violently carried off, locked up in a horrible stinking room, prevented from seeing his friends; after a day or two he is forced on board a tender, where Mr. Tripp, a midshipman, behaves with humanity, but the Captain and Lieutenant outvie each other in brutality; Captain Hamilton behaving as an 'enraged partisan.' Poor Mr. Caton is released at last by the exertions of Mr. Edmund Burke, of Mr. Farr, and another devoted friend, who travel post-haste to London to obtain a Habeas Corpus, so that he is able to write indignantly and safe from his own home to the LONDON PACKET to describe his providential escape. The little sheet gives one a vivid impression of that daily life in 1779, when Miss Edgeworth must have been a little girl of twelve years old, at school at Mrs. Lataffiere's, and learning to write in her beautiful handwriting. It was a time of great events. The world is fighting, armies marching and counter-marching, and countries rapidly changing hands. Miss Seward is inditing her elegant descriptions for the use of her admiring circle. But already the circle is dwindling! Mr. Day has parted from Sabrina. The well-known episodes of Lichfield gaieties and love-makings are over. Poor Major Andre has been exiled from England and rejected by Honora. The beautiful Honora, whose "blending charms of mind and person" are celebrated by one adoring lover after another, has married Mr. Edgeworth. She has known happiness, and the devoted affection of an adoring husband, and the admiring love of her little step-daughter, all this had been hers; and now all this is coming to an end, and the poor lady lying on her death-bed imploring her husband to marry her sister Elizabeth. Accordingly Mr. Edgeworth married Elizabeth Sneyd in 1780, which was also the year of poor Andre's death.

There is a little oval picture at the National Gallery in Dublin, the photograph of a sketch at Edgeworthstown House, which gives one a very good impression of the family as it must have appeared in the reigns of King George and the third Mrs. Edgeworth. The father in his powder and frills sits at the table with intelligent, well-informed finger showing some place upon a map. He is an agreeable-looking youngish man; Mrs. Edgeworth, his third wife, is looking over his shoulder; she has marked features, beautiful eyes, she holds a child upon her knee, and one can see the likeness in her to her step-daughter Honora, who stands just behind her and leans against the chair. A large globe appropriately stands in the background. The grown-up ladies alternate with small children. Miss Edgeworth herself, sitting opposite to her father, is the most prominent figure in the group. She wears a broad leghorn hat, a frizzed coiffure, and folded kerchief; she has a sprightly, somewhat French appearance, with a marked nose of the RETROUSSE order. I had so often heard that she was plain that to see this fashionable and agreeable figure was a pleasant surprise.

Miss Edgeworth seems to be about four-and-twenty in the sketch; she was born in 1767; she must have been eleven in 1778, when Mr. Edgeworth finally came over to Ireland to settle on his own estate, and among his own people. He had been obliged some years before to leave Edgeworthstown on account of Mrs. Honora Edgeworth's health; he now returned in patriarchal fashion with Mrs. Elizabeth Edgeworth, his third wife, with his children by his first, second, and third marriages, and with two sisters-in-law who had made their home in his family. For thirty-five years he continued to live on in the pretty old home which he now adapted to his large family, and which, notwithstanding Miss Edgeworth's objections, would have seemed so well fitted for its various requirements. The daughter's description of his life there, of his work among his tenants, of his paternal and spirited rule, is vivid and interesting. When the present owner of Edgeworthstown talked to us of his grandfather, one felt that, with all his eccentricities, he must have been a man of a far-seeing mind and observation. Mr. Erroles Edgeworth said that he was himself still reaping the benefit of his grandfather's admirable organisation and arrangements on the estate, and that when people all around met with endless difficulties and complications, he had scarcely known any. Would that there had been more Mr. Edgeworths in Ireland!

Whatever business he had to do, his daughter tells us, was done in the midst of his family. Maria copied his letters of business and helped him to receive his rents. 'On most Irish estates,' says Miss Edgeworth, 'there is, or there was, a personage commonly called a driver,—a person who drives and impounds cattle for rent and arrears.' The drivers are, alas! from time to time too necessary in collecting Irish rents. Mr. Edgeworth desired that none of his tenants should pay rent to any one but himself; thus taking away subordinate interference, he became individually acquainted with his tenantry. He also made himself acquainted with the different value of land on his estate. In every case where the tenant had improved the land his claim to preference over every new proposer was admitted. The mere plea, 'I have been on your Honour's estate so many years,' was disregarded. 'Nor was it advantageous that each son,' says Miss Edgeworth, 'of the original tenant should live on his subdivided little potato garden without further exertion of mind or body.' Further on she continues: 'Not being in want of ready money, my father was not obliged to let his land to the highest bidder. He could afford to have good tenants.' In the old leases claims of duty-fowl, of duty-work, of man or beast had been inserted. Mr. Edgeworth was one of the first to abolish them. The only clause he continued in every lease was the alienation fine, which was to protect the landlord and to prevent a set of middlemen from taking land at a reasonable rent, and letting it immediately at the highest possible price. His indulgence as to the time he allowed for the payment of rent was unusually great, but beyond the half year the tenants knew his strictness so well, that they rarely ventured to go into arrears, and never did so with impunity. 'To his character as a good landlord,' she continues, 'was added that he was a real gentleman; this phrase comprises a good deal in the opinion of the lower Irish.' There is one very curious paragraph in which Miss Edgeworth describes how her father knew how to make use of the tenants' prejudices, putting forward his wishes rather than his convictions. 'It would be impossible for me,' says his daughter, 'without ostentation to give any of the proofs I might record of my father's liberality. Long after they were forgotten by himself, they were remembered by the warm-hearted people among whom he lived.'

Mr. Edgeworth was one of those people born to get their own way. Every one seems to have felt the influence of his strong character. It was not only with his family and his friends that he held his own— the tenants and the poor people rallied to his command. To be sure, it sounds like some old Irish legend to be told that Mr. Edgeworth had so loud a voice that it could be heard a mile off, and that his steward, who lived in a lodge at that distance from the house, could hear him calling from the drawing-room window, and would come up for orders.

In 1778, says Miss Edgeworth retrospectively, when England was despatching her armies all over the world, she had no troops to spare for the defence of Ireland then threatened with a French invasion; and the principal nobility and gentry embodied themselves volunteers for the defence of the country. The Duke of Leinster and Lord Charlemont were at the head of the 'corps which in perfect order and good discipline rendered their country respectable.' The friends of Ireland, profiting by England's growing consideration for the sister country, now obtained for her great benefits for which they had long been striving, and Mr. Grattan moved an address to the throne asserting the legislative independence of Ireland. The address passed the House, and, as his daughter tells us, Mr. Edgeworth immediately published a pamphlet. Miss Edgeworth continues as follows, describing his excellent course of action: 'My father honestly and unostentatiously used his utmost endeavours to obliterate all that could tend to perpetuate ill-will in the country. Among the lower classes in his neighbourhood he endeavoured to discourage that spirit of recrimination and retaliation which the lower Irish are too prone to cherish. They are such acute observers that there is no deceiving them as to the state of the real feeling of their superiors. They know the signs of what passes within with more certainty than any physiognomist, and it was soon seen by all those who had any connection with him that my father was sincere in his disdain of vengeance.' Further on, describing his political feelings, she says that on the subject of the Union in parliamentary phrase he had not then been able to make up his mind. She describes with some pride his first speech in the Irish House at two o'clock in the morning, when the wearied members were scarcely awake to hear it, and when some of the outstretched members were aroused by their neighbours to listen to him! 'When people perceived that it was not a set speech,' says Miss Edgeworth, 'they became interested.' He stated his doubts just as they had occurred as he threw them by turn into each scale. After giving many reasons in favour of what appeared to be the advantages of the Union, he unexpectedly gave his vote against it, because he said he had been convinced by what he had heard one night, that the Union was decidedly against the wishes of the majority of men of sense and property in the nation. He added (and surely Mr. Edgeworth's opinion should go for something still) that if he should be convinced that the opinions of the country changed, his vote would be in its favour.

His biographer tells us that Mr. Edgeworth was much complimented on his speech by BOTH sides, by those for whom he voted, and also by those who found that the best arguments on the other side of the question had been undoubtedly made by him. It is a somewhat complicated statement and state of feeling to follow; to the faithful daughter nothing is impossible where her father is concerned. This vote, I believe, cost Mr. Edgeworth his peerage. 'When it was known that he had voted against the Union he became suddenly the idol of those who would previously have stoned him,' says his devoted biographer. It must not, however, be forgotten that Mr. Edgeworth had refused an offer of L3000 for his seat for two or three weeks, during that momentous period when every vote was of importance. Mr. Pitt, they say, spent over L2,000,000 in carrying the measure which he deemed so necessary.


IV


As a rule people's books appeal first to one's imagination, and then after a time, if the books are good books and alive, not stuffed dummies and reproductions, one begins to divine the writers themselves, hidden away in their pages, and wrapped up in their hot-press sheets of paper; and so it happened by chance that a printed letter once written by Maria Edgeworth to Mrs. Barbauld set the present reader wondering about these two familiar names, and trying to realise the human beings which they each represented. Since those days Miss Edgeworth has become a personage more vivid and interesting than any of her characters, more familiar even than 'Simple Susan' or 'Rosamond of the Purple Jar.' She has seemed little by little to grow into a friend, as the writer has learnt to know her more and more intimately, has visited the home of that home-loving woman, has held in her hands the delightful Family Memoirs, has seen the horizons, so to speak, of Maria Edgeworth's long life. [Now published and edited by Mr. Hare (Nov. 1894).] Several histories of Miss Edgeworth have been lately published in England. Miss Zimmern and Miss Oliver in America have each written, and the present writer has written, and various memoirs and letters have appeared in different magazines and papers with allusions and descriptions all more or less interesting. One can but admire the spirit which animated that whole existence; the cheerful, kindly, multiplied interest Maria Edgeworth took in the world outside, as well as in the wellbeing of all those around her. Generations, changes, new families, new experiences, none of these overwhelmed her. She seemed to move in a crowd, a cheerful, orderly crowd, keeping in tune and heart with its thousand claims; with strength and calmness of mind to bear multiplied sorrows and a variety of care with courage, and an ever-reviving gift of spirited interest. Her history is almost unique in its curious relationships; its changes of step-mothers, its warm family ties, its grasp of certain facts which belong to all time rather than to the hour itself. Miss Edgeworth lived for over eighty years, busy, beneficent, modest, and intelligent to the last. When she died she was mourned as unmarried women of eighty are not often mourned.

The present owner of Edgeworthstown told us that he could just remember her, lying dead upon her bed, and her face upon the pillow, and the sorrowful tears of the household; and how he and the other little children were carried off by a weeping aunt into the woods, to comfort and distract them on the funeral day. He also told us of an incident prior to this event which should not be overlooked. How he himself, being caught red-handed, at the age of four or thereabouts, with his hands in a box of sugar-plums, had immediately confessed the awful fact that he had been about to eat them, and he was brought then and there before his Aunt Maria for sentence. She at once decided that he had behaved Nobly in speaking the truth, and that he must be rewarded in kind for his praiseworthy conduct, and be allowed to keep the sugar-plums!

This little story after half a century certainly gives one pleasure still to recall, and proves, I think, that cakes may be enjoyed long after they have been eaten, and also that there is a great deal to be said for justice with lollipops in the scale. But what would Rosamond's parents have thought of such a decision? One shudders to think of their disapproval, or of that of dear impossible Mr. Thomas Day, with his trials and experiments of melted sealing-wax upon little girls' bare arms, and his glasses of tar-water so inflexibly administered. Miss Edgeworth, who suffered from her eyes, recalls how Mr. Day used to bring the dose, the horrible tar-water, every morning with a 'Drink this, Miss Maria!' and how she dared not resist, though she thought she saw something of kindness and pity beneath all his apparent severity.

Severity was the order of those times. The reign of sugar-plums had scarcely begun. It was not, as now, only ignorance and fanaticism that encouraged the giving of pain, it was the universal custom. People were still hanged for stealing, women were still burnt—so we have been assured—in St. Stephen's Green; though, it is true, they were considerately strangled first. Children were bullied and tortured with the kindest intentions; even Maria Edgeworth at her fashionable school was stretched in a sort of machine to make her grow; Mr. Day, as we know, to please the lady of his affections, passed eight hours a day in the stocks in order to turn out his knock-knees. One feels that a generation of ladies and gentlemen who submitted to such inflictions surely belonged to a race of heroes and heroines, and that, if the times were difficult and trying, the people also were stronger to endure them, and must have been much better fitted with nerves than we are.

Miss Edgeworth's life has been so often told that I will not attempt to recapitulate the story at any length. She well deserved her reputation. Her thoughts were good, her English was good, her stories had the charm of sincerity, and her audience of children was a genuine audience, less likely to be carried away by fashion than more advanced critics might be. There is a curious matter-of-fact element in all she wrote, combined with extraordinary quickness and cleverness; and it must be remembered, in trying to measure her place in literature, that in her day the whole great school of English philosophical romance was in its cradle; George Eliot was not in existence; my father was born in the year in which THE ABSENTEE was published. Sir Walter Scott has told us that it was Miss Edgeworth's writing which first suggested to him the idea of writing about Scotland and its national life. Tourgenieff in the same way says that it was after reading her books on Ireland that he began to write of his own country and of Russian peasants as he did. Miss Edgeworth was the creator of her own special world of fiction, though the active Mr. Edgeworth crossed the t's and dotted the i's, interpolated, expurgated, to his own and Maria's satisfaction. She was essentially a modest woman; she gratefully accepted his criticism and emendations. Mr. Clark Russell quotes Sydney Smith, who declared that Mr. Edgeworth must have written or burst. 'A discharge of ink was an evacuation absolutely necessary to avoid fatal and plethoric congestion.' The only wonder is that, considering all they went through, his daughter's stories survived to tell their tale, and to tell it so well, with directness and conviction, that best of salt in any literary work. A letter Maria wrote to her cousin will be remembered. 'I beg, dear Sophy,' she says, 'that you will not call my stories by the sublime name of my works; I shall else be ashamed when the little mouse comes forth.'

Maria's correspondence is delightful, and conveys us right away into that bygone age. The figures rapidly move across her scene, talking and unconsciously describing themselves as they go; you see them all through the eyes of the observant little lady. She did not go very deep; she seems to me to have made kindly acquaintance with some, to have admired others with artless enthusiasm. I don't think she troubled herself much about complication of feeling; she liked people to make repartees, or to invent machines, to pay their bills, and to do their duty in a commonplace and cheerfully stoical fashion. But then Maria Edgeworth certainly did not belong to our modern schools, sipping the emetic goblet to give flavour to daily events, nor to that still more alarming and spreading clique of DEGENERES who insist upon administering such doses to others to relieve the tedium of the road of life.

Perhaps we in our time scarcely do justice to Miss Edgeworth's extraordinary cleverness and brightness of apprehension. There is more fun than humour in her work, and those were the days of good rollicking jokes and laughter. Details change so quickly that it is almost impossible to grasp entirely the aims and intentions of a whole set of people just a little different from ourselves in every single thing; who held their heads differently, who pointed their toes differently, who addressed each other in a language just a little unlike our own. The very meanings of the words shift from one generation to another, and we are perhaps more really in harmony with our great-great-grandfathers than with the more immediate generations.

Her society was charming, so every one agrees; and her acquaintance with all the most remarkable men of her time must not be forgotten, nor the genuine regard with which she inspired all who came across her path.

'In external appearance she is quite the fairy of our nursery tale, the WHIPPETY STOURIE, if you remember such a sprite, who came flying through the window to work all sorts of marvels,' writes Sir Walter. 'I will never believe but what she has a wand in her pocket, and pulls it out to conjure a little before she begins those very striking pictures of manners.'

Among others Sir William Hamilton has left a pleasing description of Miss Edgeworth. 'If you would study and admire her as she deserves, you must see her at home,' says he, 'and hear her talk. She knows an infinite number of anecdotes about interesting places and persons, which she tells extremely well, and never except when they arise naturally out of the subject. . . . To crown her merits, she seemed to take a prodigious fancy to me, and promised to be at home, and made me promise to be at Edgeworthstown for a fortnight some time next vacation.' We owe to him also an amusing sketch of some other collateral members of the family; the fine animated old lady, who immediately gets him to explain the reason why a concave mirror inverts while a convex mirror leaves them erect; the young ladies, one of whom was particularly anxious to persuade him that the roundness of the planets was produced by friction, perhaps by their being shaken together like marbles in a bag.

There is also an interesting letter from Sir W. Hamilton at Edgeworthstown on 23rd September 1829. Wordsworth is also staying there. 'After some persuasion Francis and I succeed in engaging Mr. Wordsworth in many very interesting conversations. Miss Edgeworth has had for some time a very serious illness, but she was able to join us for dinner the day that I arrived, and she exhibited in her conversations with Mr. Wordsworth a good deal of her usual brilliancy; she also engaged Mr. Marshall in some long conversations upon Ireland, and even Mr. Marshall's son, whose talent for silence seems to be so very profound, was thawed a little on Monday evening, and discussed after tea the formation of the solar system. Miss Edgeworth tells me that she is at last employed in writing for the public after a long interval, but does not expect to have her work soon ready for publication.' [There is a curious criticism of Miss Edgeworth by Robert Hall, the great preacher, which should not be passed over. 'As to her style,' he says, 'she is simple and elegant, content to convey her thoughts in their most plain and natural form, that is indeed the perfection of style. . . . In point of tendency,' he continues, 'I should class her books among the most irreligious I ever read. . . . She does not attack religion nor inveigh against it, but makes it appear unnecessary by exhibiting perfect virtue without it. . . . No works ever produced so bad an effect on my own mind as hers.']

Besides Wordsworth and Sir William Hamilton and Mr. Marshall, we presently come to Sir John Herschell. 'I saw your admirable friend Miss Edgeworth lately in town,' he writes to Hamilton; 'she is a most warm admirer of yours, and praise such as hers is what any man might be proud of.' Later on Miss Edgeworth, corresponding with Sir W. Hamilton, tells him she is ill and forbidden to write, or even to think. This is what she thinks of THINKING: 'I am glad to see that the severe sciences do not destroy the energy and grace of the imagination, but only chasten it and impart their philosophical influence.'

V

Certain events are remembered and mourned for generations, so there are others, happy and interesting in themselves, which must continue to give satisfaction long after they are over, and long after those concerned in them have passed away. And certainly among things pleasant to remember is the story of Sir Walter Scott's visit to Ireland in July 1825, when he received so warm a greeting from the country and spent those happy hours with Miss Edgeworth at Edgeworthstown. Fortunately for us, Lockhart was one of the party. Anne Scott, and Walter the soldier, and Jane Scott the bride, were also travelling in Sir Walter's train. The reception which Ireland gave Sir Walter was a warm-hearted ovation. 'It would be endless to enumerate the distinguished persons who, morning after morning, crowded to his levee in St. Stephen's Green,' says Lockhart, and he quotes an old saying of Sir Robert Peel's, 'that Sir Walter's reception in the High Street of Edinburgh is 1822 was the first thing that gave him (Peel) a notion of the electric shock of a nation's gratitude.' 'I doubt if even that scene surpassed what I myself witnessed,' continues the biographer, 'when Sir Walter returned down Dame Street after inspecting the Castle of Dublin.'

From ovations to friendship it was Sir Walter's inclination to turn. On the 1st August he came to Edgeworthstown, accompanied by his family. 'We remained there for several days, making excursions to Loch Oel, etc. Mr. Lovell Edgeworth had his classical mansion filled every evening with a succession of distinguished friends. Here, above all, we had the opportunity of seeing in what universal respect and comfort a gentleman's family may live in that country, provided only they live there habitually and do their duty. . . . Here we found neither mud hovels nor naked peasantry, but snug cottages and smiling faces all about. . . . Here too we pleased ourselves with recognising some of the sweetest features in Goldsmith's picture of "Sweet Auburn! loveliest village of the plain."' Oliver Goldsmith received his education at this very school of Edgeworthstown, and Pallas More, the little hamlet where the author of THE VICAR OF WAKEFIELD first saw the light, is still, as it was then, the property of the Edgeworths.

So Scott came to visit his little friend, and the giant was cheered and made welcome by her charming hospitality. It was a last gleam of sunshine in that noble life. We instinctively feel how happy they all were in each other's good company. We can almost overhear some of their talk, as they walk together under the shade of the trees of the park. One can imagine him laughing in his delightful hearty way, half joking, half caressing. Lockhart had used some phrase (it is Lockhart who tells us the story) which conveyed the impression that he suspects poets and novelists of looking at life and at the world chiefly as materials for art. 'A soft and pensive shade came over Scott's face. "I fear you have some very young ideas in your head," he says. "God help us, what a poor world this would be if that were the true doctrine! I have read books enough, and observed and conversed with enough eminent minds in my time, but I assure you I have heard higher sentiments from the lips of poor uneducated men and women, exerting the spirit of severe yet gentle heroism, or speaking their simple thoughts, than I ever met with out of the pages of the Bible. We shall never learn to feel and respect our real calling unless we have taught ourselves to consider everything as moonshine compared with the education of the heart,"' said the great teacher. 'Maria did not listen to this without some water in her eyes,—her tears are always ready when a generous string is touched,—but she brushed them gaily aside, and said, "You see how it is: Dean Swift said he had written his books in order that people should learn to treat him like a great lord; Sir Walter writes his in order that he might be able to treat his people as a great lord ought to do."'

Years and years afterwards Edward Fitzgerald stayed at Edgeworthstown, and he also carries us there in one of his letters. He had been at college with Mr. Frank Edgeworth, who had succeeded to the estate, and had now in 1828 come to stay with him. The host had been called away, but the guest describes his many hostesses: 'Edgeworth's mother, aged seventy-four; his sister, the great Maria, aged seventy-two; and another cousin or something. All these people were pleasant and kind, the house pleasant, the grounds ditto, a good library, so here I am quite at home, but surely must go to England soon.' One can imagine Fitzgerald sitting in the library with his back to the window and writing his letters and reading his thirty-two sets of novels, while the rain is steadily pouring outside, and the Great Authoress (so he writes her down) as busy as a bee sitting by chattering and making a catalogue of her books. 'We talk about Walter Scott, whom she adores, and are merry all day long,' he says. 'When I began this letter I thought I had something to say, but I believe the truth was I had nothing to do.'

Two years later Mr. Fitzgerald is again there and writing to Frederick Tennyson: 'I set sail from Dublin to-morrow night, bearing the heartfelt regrets of all the people of Ireland with me.' Then comes a flash of his kind searching lantern: 'I had a pleasant week with Edgeworth. He farms and is a justice, and goes to sleep on the sofa of evenings. At odd moments he looks into Spinoza and Petrarch. People respect him very much in these parts.' Edward Fitzgerald seems to have had a great regard for his host; the more he knows him the more he cares for him; he describes him 'firing away about the odes of Pindar.' They fired noble broadsides those men of the early Victorian times, and when we listen we still seem to hear their echoes rolling into the far distance. Mr. Fitzgerald ends his letter with a foreboding too soon to be realised: 'Old Miss Edgeworth is wearing away. She has a capital bright soul, which even now shines quite youthfully through her faded carcase.' It was in May 1849 that Maria Edgeworth went to her rest. She died almost suddenly, with no long suffering, in the arms of her faithful friend and step-mother.

In 1799, When Maria was in London, she and her father went to call upon Mr. Johnson, the bookseller, who was then imprisoned in the King's Bench for a publication which was considered to be treasonable, and they probably then and there arranged with him for the publication of CASTLE RACKRENT, for in January 1800, writing to her cousin, Miss Ruxton, Maria says, 'Will you tell me what means you have of getting parcels from London to Arundel, because I wish to send my aunt a few popular tales. . . . We have begged Johnson to send CASTLE RACKRENT, and hope it has reached you. DO NOT MENTION THAT IT IS OURS.'

The second edition of CASTLE RACKRENT came out with Miss Edgeworth's name to it in 1811. 'Its success was so triumphant,' Mrs. Edgeworth writes, 'that some one—I heard his name at the time, but do not now remember it—not only asserted that he was the author, but actually took the trouble to copy out several chapters with corrections and erasions as if it was his original manuscript.'

It was when Miss Edgeworth first came to Ireland,—so she tells one of her correspondents,—that she met the original Thady of CASTLE RACKRENT. His character struck her very much, and the story came into her mind. She purposely added to the agent's age so as to give time for the events to happen.

Honest Thady tells the story; you can almost hear his voice, and see him as he stands: 'I wear a long greatcoat winter and summer, which is very handy, as I never put my arms into the sleeves; they are as good as new, though come Holantide next I've had it these seven years: it holds on by a single button round my neck, cloak fashion. To look at me, you would hardly think "Poor Thady" was the father of Attorney Quirk; he is a high gentleman, and never minds what poor Thady says, and having better than fifteen hundred a year landed estate, looks down upon honest Thady; but I wash my hands of his doings, and as I have lived, so will I die, true and loyal to the family. The family of Rackrents is, I am proud to say, one of the most ancient in the kingdom.' And then he gives the history of the Rackrents, beginning with Sir Patrick, who could sit out the best man in Ireland, let alone the three kingdoms itself, and who fitted up the chicken-house to accommodate his friends when they honoured him unexpectedly with their company. There was 'such a fine whillaluh at Sir Patrick's funeral, you might have heard it to the farthest end of the county, and happy the man who could get but a sight of the hearse.' Then came Sir Murtagh, who used to boast that he had a law-suit for every letter in the alphabet. 'He dug up a fairy-mount against my advice,' says Thady, 'and had no luck afterwards. . . . Sir Murtagh in his passion broke a blood-vessel, and all the law in the land could do nothing in that case. . . . My lady had a fine jointure settled upon her, and took herself away, to the great joy of the tenantry. I never said anything one way or the other,' says Thady, 'whilst she was part of the family, but got up to see her go at three o'clock in the morning. "It's a fine morning, honest Thady," says she; "good-bye to ye," and into the carriage she stepped, without a word more, good or bad, or even half-a-crown, but I made my bow, and stood to see her safe out of sight for the sake of the family.'

How marvellously vivid it all is! every word tells as the generations pass before us. The very spirit of romantic Irish fidelity is incarnate in Thady. Jason Quirk represents the feline element, which also belongs to our extraordinary Celtic race. The little volume contains the history of a nation. It is a masterpiece which Miss Edgeworth has never surpassed. It is almost provoking to have so many details of other and less interesting stories, such as EARLY LESSONS, A KNAPSACK, THE PRUSSIAN VASE, etc., and to hear so little of these two books by which she will be best remembered.

## AUTHOR'S PREFACE

The Prevailing taste of the public for anecdote has been censured and ridiculed by critics who aspire to the character of superior wisdom; but if we consider it in a proper point of view, this taste is an incontestable proof of the good sense and profoundly philosophic temper of the present times. Of the numbers who study, or at least who read history, how few derive any advantage from their labours! The heroes of history are so decked out by the fine fancy of the professed historian; they talk in such measured prose, and act from such sublime or such diabolical motives, that few have sufficient taste, wickedness, or heroism, to sympathise in their fate. Besides, there is much uncertainty even in the best authenticated ancient or modern histories; and that love of truth, which in some minds is innate and immutable, necessarily leads to a love of secret memoirs and private anecdotes. We cannot judge either of the feelings or of the characters of men with perfect accuracy, from their actions or their appearance in public; it is from their careless conversations, their half-finished sentences, that we may hope with the greatest probability of success to discover their real characters. The life of a great or of a little man written by himself, the familiar letters, the diary of any individual published by his friends or by his enemies, after his decease, are esteemed important literary curiosities. We are surely justified, in this eager desire, to collect the most minute facts relative to the domestic lives, not only of the great and good, but even of the worthless and insignificant, since it is only by a comparison of their actual happiness or misery in the privacy of domestic life that we can form a just estimate of the real reward of virtue, or the real punishment of vice. That the great are not as happy as they seem, that the external circumstances of fortune and rank do not constitute felicity, is asserted by every moralist: the historian can seldom, consistently with his dignity, pause to illustrate this truth; it is therefore to the biographer we must have recourse. After we have beheld splendid characters playing their parts on the great theatre of the world, with all the advantages of stage effect and decoration, we anxiously beg to be admitted behind the scenes, that we may take a nearer view of the actors and actresses.

Some may perhaps imagine that the value of biography depends upon the judgment and taste of the biographer; but on the contrary it may be maintained, that the merits of a biographer are inversely as the extent of his intellectual powers and of his literary talents. A plain unvarnished tale is preferable to the most highly ornamented narrative. Where we see that a man has the power, we may naturally suspect that he has the will to deceive us; and those who are used to literary manufacture know how much is often sacrificed to the rounding of a period, or the pointing of an antithesis.

That the ignorant may have their prejudices as well as the learned cannot be disputed; but we see and despise vulgar errors: we never bow to the authority of him who has no great name to sanction his absurdities. The partiality which blinds a biographer to the defects of his hero, in proportion as it is gross, ceases to be dangerous; but if it be concealed by the appearance of candour, which men of great abilities best know how to assume, it endangers our judgment sometimes, and sometimes our morals. If her Grace the Duchess of Newcastle, instead of penning her lord's elaborate eulogium, had undertaken to write the life of Savage, we should not have been in any danger of mistaking an idle, ungrateful libertine for a man of genius and virtue. The talents of a biographer are often fatal to his reader. For these reasons the public often judiciously countenance those who, without sagacity to discriminate character, without elegance of style to relieve the tediousness of narrative, without enlargement of mind to draw any conclusions from the facts they relate, simply pour forth anecdotes, and retail conversations, with all the minute prolixity of a gossip in a country town.

The author of the following Memoirs has upon these grounds fair claims to the public favour and attention; he was an illiterate old steward, whose partiality to THE FAMILY, in which he was bred and born, must be obvious to the reader. He tells the history of the Rackrent family in his vernacular idiom, and in the full confidence that Sir Patrick, Sir Murtagh, Sir Kit, and Sir Condy Rackrent's affairs will be as interesting to all the world as they were to himself. Those who were acquainted with the manners of a certain class of the gentry of Ireland some years ago, will want no evidence of the truth of honest Thady's narrative; to those who are totally unacquainted with Ireland, the following Memoirs will perhaps be scarcely intelligible, or probably they may appear perfectly incredible. For the information of the IGNORANT English reader, a few notes have been subjoined by the editor, and he had it once in contemplation to translate the language of Thady into plain English; but Thady's idiom is incapable of translation, and, besides, the authenticity of his story would have been more exposed to doubt if it were not told in his own characteristic manner. Several years ago he related to the editor the history of the Rackrent family, and it was with some difficulty that he was persuaded to have it committed to writing; however, his feelings for 'THE HONOUR OF THE FAMILY,' as he expressed himself, prevailed over his habitual laziness, and he at length completed the narrative which is now laid before the public.

The editor hopes his readers will observe that these are 'tales of other times;' that the manners depicted in the following pages are not those of the present age; the race of the Rackrents has long since been extinct in Ireland; and the drunken Sir Patrick, the litigious Sir Murtagh, the fighting Sir Kit, and the slovenly Sir Condy, are characters which could no more be met with at present in Ireland, than Squire Western or Parson Trulliber in England. There is a time when individuals can bear to be rallied for their past follies and absurdities, after they have acquired new habits and a new consciousness. Nations, as well as individuals, gradually lose attachment to their identity, and the present generation is amused, rather than offended, by the ridicule that is thrown upon its ancestors.

Probably we shall soon have it in our power, in a hundred instances, to verify the truth of these observations.

When Ireland loses her identity by an union with Great Britain, she will look back, with a smile of good-humoured complacency, on the Sir Kits and Sir Condys of her former existence.

1800.

## MONDAY MORNING *[GLOSSARY 1]*

Having, out of friendship for the family, upon whose estate, praised be Heaven! I and mine have lived rent-free time out of mind, voluntarily undertaken to publish the MEMOIRS OF THE RACKRENT FAMILY, I think it my duty to say a few words, in the first place, concerning myself. My real name is Thady Quirk, though in the family I have always been known by no other than 'Honest Thady,' afterward, in the time of Sir Murtagh, deceased, I remember to hear them calling me 'Old Thady,' and now I've come to 'Poor Thady'; for I wear a long greatcoat winter and summer, which is very handy, as I never put my arms into the sleeves; they are as good as new, though come Holantide next I've had it these seven years: it holds on by a single button round my neck, cloak fashion.

[The cloak, or mantle, as described by Thady, is of high antiquity. Spenser, in his VIEW OF THE STATE OF IRELAND, proves that it is not, as some have imagined, peculiarly derived from the Scythians, but that 'most nations of the world anciently used the mantle; for the Jews used it, as you may read of Elias's mantle, etc.; the Chaldees also used it, as you may read in Diodorus; the Egyptians likewise used it, as you may read in Herodotus, and may be gathered by the description of Berenice in the Greek Commentary upon Callimachus; the Greeks also used it anciently, as appeared by Venus's mantle lined with stars, though afterward they changed the form thereof into their cloaks, called Pallai, as some of the Irish also use; and the ancient Latins and Romans used it, as you may read in Virgil, who was a great antiquary, that Evander, when AEneas came to him at his feast, did entertain and feast him sitting on the ground, and lying on mantles: insomuch that he useth the very word mantile for a mantle—

"Humi mantilia sternunt:"

so that it seemeth that the mantle was a general habit to most nations, and not proper to the Scythians only.

Spenser knew the convenience of the said mantle, as housing, bedding, and clothing: 'IREN. Because the commodity doth not countervail the discommodity; for the inconveniences which thereby do arise are much more many; for it is a fit house for an outlaw, a meet bed for a rebel, and an apt cloak for a thief. First, the outlaw being, for his many crimes and villanies, banished from the towns and houses of honest men, and wandering in waste places, far from danger of law, maketh his mantle his house, and under it covereth himself from the wrath of Heaven, from the offence of the earth, and from the sight of men. When it raineth, it is his penthouse; when it bloweth, it is his tent; when it freezeth, it is his tabernacle. In summer he can wear it loose; in winter he can wrap it close; at all times he can use it; never heavy, never cumbersome. Likewise for a rebel it is as serviceable; for in this war that he maketh (if at least it deserves the name of war), when he still flieth from his foe, and lurketh in the THICK WOODS (this should be BLACK BOGS) and straight passages, waiting for advantages, it is his bed, yea, and almost his household stuff.']

To look at me, you would hardly think 'Poor Thady' was the father of Attorney Quirk; he is a high gentleman, and never minds what poor Thady says, and having better than fifteen hundred a year, landed estate, looks down upon honest Thady; but I wash my hands of his doings, and as I have lived so will I die, true and loyal to the family. The family of the Rackrents is, I am proud to say, one of the most ancient in the kingdom. Everybody knows this is not the old family name, which was O'Shaughlin, related to the kings of Ireland—but that was before my time. My grandfather was driver to the great Sir Patrick O'Shaughlin, and I heard him, when I was a boy, telling how the Castle Rackrent estate came to Sir Patrick; Sir Tallyhoo Rackrent was cousin-german to him, and had a fine estate of his own, only never a gate upon it, it being his maxim that a car was the best gate. Poor gentleman! he lost a fine hunter and his life, at last, by it, all in one day's hunt. But I ought to bless that day, for the estate came straight into THE family, upon one condition, which Sir Patrick O'Shaughlin at the time took sadly to heart, they say, but thought better of it afterwards, seeing how large a stake depended upon it: that he should, by Act of Parliament, take and bear the surname and arms of Rackrent.

Now it was that the world was to see what was IN Sir Patrick. On coming into the estate he gave the finest entertainment ever was heard of in the country; not a man could stand after supper but Sir Patrick himself who could sit out the best man in Ireland, let alone the three kingdoms itself [GLOSSARY 2]. He had his house, from one year's end to another, as full of company as ever it could hold, and fuller; for rather than be left out of the parties at Castle Rackrent, many gentlemen, and those men of the first consequence and landed estates in the country—such as the O'Neills of Ballynagrotty, and the Moneygawls of Mount Juliet's Town, and O'Shannons of New Town Tullyhog—made it their choice, often and often, when there was no room to be had for love nor money, in long winter nights, to sleep in the chicken-house, which Sir Patrick had fitted up for the purpose of accommodating his friends and the public in general, who honoured him with their company unexpectedly at Castle Rackrent; and this went on I can't tell you how long. The whole country rang with his praises!—long life to him! I'm sure I love to look upon his picture, now opposite to me; though I never saw him, he must have been a portly gentleman—his neck something short, and remarkable for the largest pimple on his nose, which, by his particular desire, is still extant in his picture, said to be a striking likeness, though taken when young. He is said also to be the inventor of raspberry whisky, which is very likely, as nobody has ever appeared to dispute it with him, and as there still exists a broken punch-bowl at Castle Rackrent, in the garret, with an inscription to that effect—a great curiosity. A few days before his death he was very merry; it being his honour's birthday, he called my grandfather in—God bless him!—to drink the company's health, and filled a bumper himself, but could not carry it to his head, on account of the great shake in his hand; on this he cast his joke, saying, 'What would my poor father say to me if he was to pop out of the grave, and see me now? I remember when I was a little boy, the first bumper of claret he gave me after dinner, how he praised me for carrying it so steady to my mouth. Here's my thanks to him—a bumper toast.' Then he fell to singing the favourite song he learned from his father—for the last time, poor gentleman—he sung it that night as loud and as hearty as ever, with a chorus:

He that goes to bed, and goes to bed sober,
Falls as the leaves do, falls as the leaves do, and dies in October;
'But he that goes to bed, and goes to bed mellow,
Lives as he ought to do, lives as he ought to do, and dies an honest fellow.

Sir Patrick died that night: just as the company rose to drink his health with three cheers, he fell down in a sort of fit, and was carried off; they sat it out, and were surprised, on inquiry in the morning, to find that it was all over with poor Sir Patrick. Never did any gentleman live and die more beloved in the country by rich and poor. His funeral was such a one as was never known before or since in the county! All the gentlemen in the three counties were at it; far and near, how they flocked! my great-grandfather said, that to see all the women, even in their red cloaks, you would have taken them for the army drawn out. Then such a fine whillaluh! [*GLOSSARY 3*] you might have heard it to the farthest end of the county, and happy the man who could get but a sight of the hearse! But who'd have thought it? Just as all was going on right, through his own town they were passing, when the body was seized for debt—a rescue was apprehended from the mob; but the heir, who attended the funeral, was against that, for fear of consequences, seeing that those villains who came to serve acted under the disguise of the law: so, to be sure, the law must take its course, and little gain had the creditors for their pains. First and foremost, they had the curses of the country: and Sir Murtagh Rackrent, the new heir, in the next place, on account of this affront to the body, refused to pay a shilling of the debts, in which he was countenanced by all the best gentlemen of property, and others of his acquaintance; Sir Murtagh alleging in all companies that he all along meant to pay his father's debts of honour, but the moment the law was taken of him, there was an end of honour to be sure. It was whispered (but none but the enemies of the family believe it) that this was all a sham seizure to get quit of the debts which he had bound himself to pay in honour.

It's a long time ago, there's no saying how it was, but this for certain, the new man did not take at all after the old gentleman; the cellars were never filled after his death, and no open house, or anything as it used to be; the tenants even were sent away without their whisky [GLOSSARY 4]. I was ashamed myself, and knew not what to say for the honour of the family; but I made the best of a bad case, and laid it all at my lady's door, for I did not like her anyhow, nor anybody else; she was of the family of the Skinflints, and a widow; it was a strange match for Sir Murtagh; the people in the country thought he demeaned himself greatly [GLOSSARY 5], but I said nothing; I knew how it was. Sir Murtagh was a great lawyer, and looked to the great Skinflint estate; there, however, he overshot himself; for though one of the co-heiresses, he was never the better for her, for she outlived him many's the long day—he could not see that to be sure when he married her. I must say for her, she made him the best of wives, being a very notable, stirring woman, and looking close to everything. But I always suspected she had Scotch blood in her veins; anything else I could have looked over in her, from a regard to the family. She was a strict observer, for self and servants, of Lent, and all fast-days, but not holidays. One of the maids having fainted three times the last day of Lent, to keep soul and body together, we put a morsel of roast beef into her mouth, which came from Sir Murtagh's dinner, who never fasted, not he; but somehow or other it unfortunately reached my lady's ears, and the priest of the parish had a complaint made of it the next day, and the poor girl was forced, as soon as she could walk, to do penance for it, before she could get any peace or absolution, in the house or out of it. However, my lady was very charitable in her own way. She had a charity school for poor children, where they were taught to read and write gratis, and where they were kept well to spinning gratis for my lady in return; for she had always heaps of duty yarn from the tenants, and got all her household linen out of the estate from first to last; for after the spinning, the weavers on the estate took it in hand for nothing, because of the looms my lady's interest could get from the Linen Board to distribute gratis. Then there was a bleach-yard near us, and the tenant dare refuse my lady nothing, for fear of a lawsuit Sir Murtagh kept hanging over him about the watercourse. With these ways of managing, 'tis surprising how cheap my lady got things done, and how proud she was of it. Her table the same way, kept for next to nothing [GLOSSARY 6]; duty fowls, and duty turkeys, and duty geese, came as fast as we could eat 'em, for my lady kept a sharp lookout, and knew to a tub of butter everything the tenants had, all round. They knew her way, and what with fear of driving for rent and Sir Murtagh's lawsuits, they were kept in such good order, they never thought of coming near Castle Rackrent without a present of something or other—nothing too much or too little for my lady—eggs, honey, butter, meal, fish, game, grouse, and herrings, fresh or salt, all went for something. As for their young pigs, we had them, and the best bacon and hams they could make up, with all young chickens in spring; but they were a set of poor wretches, and we had nothing but misfortunes with them, always breaking and running away. This, Sir Murtagh and my lady said, was all their former landlord Sir Patrick's fault, who let 'em all get the half-year's rent into arrear; there was something in that to be sure. But Sir Murtagh was as much the contrary way; for let alone making English tenants [GLOSSARY 7] of them, every soul, he was always driving and driving, and pounding and pounding, and canting and canting [GLOSSARY 8], and replevying and replevying, and he made a good living of trespassing cattle; there was always some tenant's pig, or horse, or cow, or calf, or goose, trespassing, which was so great a gain to Sir Murtagh, that he did not like to hear me talk of repairing fences. Then his heriots and duty-work [GLOSSARY 9] brought him in something, his turf was cut, his potatoes set and dug, his hay brought home, and, in short, all the work about his house done for nothing; for in all our leases there were strict clauses heavy with penalties, which Sir Murtagh knew well how to enforce; so many days' duty-work of man and horse, from every tenant, he was to have, and had, every year; and when a man vexed him, why, the finest day he could pitch on, when the cratur was getting in his own harvest, or thatching his cabin, Sir Murtagh made it a principle to call upon him and his horse; so he taught 'em all, as he said, to know the law of landlord and tenant. As for law, I believe no man, dead or alive, ever loved it so well as Sir Murtagh. He had once sixteen suits pending at a time, and I never saw him so much himself: roads, lanes, bogs, wells, ponds, eel-wires, orchards, trees, tithes, vagrants, gravelpits, sandpits, dunghills, and nuisances, everything upon the face of the earth furnished him good matter for a suit. He used to boast that he had a lawsuit for every letter in the alphabet. How I used to wonder to see Sir Murtagh in the midst of the papers in his office! Why, he could hardly turn about for them. I made bold to shrug my shoulders once in his presence, and thanked my stars I was not born a gentleman to so much toil and trouble; but Sir Murtagh took me up short with his old proverb, 'learning is better than house or land.' Out of forty-nine suits which he had, he never lost one but seventeen [*GLOSSARY 10*]; the rest he gained with costs, double costs, treble costs sometimes; but even that did not pay. He was a very learned man in the law, and had the character of it; but how it was I can't tell, these suits that he carried cost him a power of money: in the end he sold some hundreds a year of the family estate; but he was a very learned man in the law, and I know nothing of the matter, except having a great regard for the family; and I could not help grieving when he sent me to post up notices of the sale of the fee simple of the lands and appurtenances of Timoleague.

'I know, honest Thady,' says he, to comfort me, 'what I'm about better than you do; I'm only selling to get the ready money wanting to carry on my suit with spirit with the Nugents of Carrickashaughlin.'

He was very sanguine about that suit with the Nugents of Carrickashaughlin. He could have gained it, they say, for certain, had it pleased Heaven to have spared him to us, and it would have been at the least a plump two thousand a year in his way; but things were ordered otherwise—for the best to be sure. He dug up a fairy-mount against my advice, and had no luck afterwards. [These fairy-mounts are called ant-hills in England. They are held in high reverence by the common people in Ireland. A gentleman, who in laying out his lawn had occasion to level one of these hillocks, could not prevail upon any of his labourers to begin the ominous work. He was obliged to take a LOY from one of their reluctant hands, and began the attack himself. The labourers agreed that the vengeance of the fairies would fall upon the head of the presumptuous mortal who first disturbed them in their retreat [*GLOSSARY 11*].] Though a learned man in the law, he was a little too incredulous in other matters. I warned him that I heard the very Banshee that my grandfather heard under Sir Patrick's window a few days before his death. [The Banshee is a species of aristocratic fairy, who, in the shape of a little hideous old woman, has been known to appear, and heard to sing in a mournful supernatural voice under the windows of great houses, to warn the family that some of them are soon to die. In the last century every great family in Ireland had a Banshee, who attended regularly; but latterly their visits and songs have been discontinued.] But Sir Murtagh thought nothing of the Banshee, nor of his cough, with a spitting of blood, brought on, I understand, by catching cold in attending the courts, and overstraining his chest with making himself heard in one of his favourite causes. He was a great speaker with a powerful voice; but his last speech was not in the courts at all. He and my lady, though both of the same way of thinking in some things, and though she was as good a wife and great economist as you could see, and he the best of husbands, as to looking into his affairs, and making money for his family; yet I don't know how it was, they had a great deal of sparring and jarring between them. My lady had her privy purse; and she had her weed ashes [*GLOSSARY 12*], and her sealing money [*GLOSSARY 13*] upon the signing of all the leases, with something to buy gloves besides; and, besides, again often took money from the tenants, if offered properly, to speak for them to Sir Murtagh about abatements and renewals. Now the weed ashes and the glove money he allowed her clear perquisites; though once when he saw her in a new gown saved out of the weed ashes, he told her to my face (for he could say a sharp thing) that she should not put on her weeds before her husband's death. But in a dispute about an abatement my lady would have the last word, and Sir Murtagh grew mad [*GLOSSARY 14*]; I was within hearing of the door, and now I wish I had made bold to step in. He spoke so loud, the whole kitchen was out on the stairs [*GLOSSARY 15*]. All on a sudden he stopped, and my lady too. Something has surely happened, thought I; and so it was, for Sir Murtagh in his passion broke a blood-vessel, and all the law in the land could do nothing in that case. My lady sent for five physicians, but Sir Murtagh died, and was buried. She had a fine jointure settled upon her, and took herself away, to the great joy of the tenantry. I never said anything one way or the other whilst she was part of the family, but got up to see her go at three o'clock in the morning.

'It's a fine morning, honest Thady,' says she; 'good-bye to ye.' And into the carriage she stepped, without a word more, good or bad, or even half-a-crown; but I made my bow, and stood to see her safe out of sight for the sake of the family.

Then we were all bustle in the house, which made me keep out of the way, for I walk slow and hate a bustle; but the house was all hurry-skurry, preparing for my new master. Sir Murtagh, I forgot to notice, had no childer [CHILDER: this is the manner in which many of Thady's rank, and others in Ireland, formerly pronounced the word CHILDREN]; so the Rackrent estate went to his younger brother, a young dashing officer, who came amongst us before I knew for the life of me whereabouts I was, in a gig or some of them things, with another spark along with him, and led horses, and servants, and dogs, and scarce a place to put any Christian of them into; for my late lady had sent all the feather-beds off before her, and blankets and household linen, down to the very knife-cloths, on the cars to Dublin, which were all her own, lawfully paid for out of her own money. So the house was quite bare, and my young master, the moment ever he set foot in it out of his gig, thought all those things must come of themselves, I believe, for he never looked after anything at all, but harum-scarum called for everything as if we were conjurors, or he in a public-house. For my part, I could not bestir myself anyhow; I had been so much used to my late master and mistress, all was upside down with me, and the new servants in the servants' hall were quite out of my way; I had nobody to talk to, and if it had not been for my pipe and tobacco, should, I verily believe, have broke my heart for poor Sir Murtagh.

But one morning my new master caught a glimpse of me as I was looking at his horse's heels, in hopes of a word from him. 'And is that old Thady?' says he, as he got into his gig: I loved him from that day to this, his voice was so like the family; and he threw me a guinea out of his waistcoat-pocket, as he drew up the reins with the other hand, his horse rearing too; I thought I never set my eyes on a finer figure of a man, quite another sort from Sir Murtagh, though withal, TO ME, a family likeness. A fine life we should have led, had he stayed amongst us, God bless him! He valued a guinea as little as any man: money to him was no more than dirt, and his gentleman and groom, and all belonging to him, the same; but the sporting season over, he grew tired of the place, and having got down a great architect for the house, and an improver for the grounds, and seen their plans and elevations, he fixed a day for settling with the tenants, but went off in a whirlwind to town, just as some of them came into the yard in the morning. A circular letter came next post from the new agent, with news that the master was sailed for England, and he must remit L500 to Bath for his use before a fortnight was at an end; bad news still for the poor tenants, no change still for the better with them. Sir Kit Rackrent, my young master, left all to the agent; and though he had the spirit of a prince, and lived away to the honour of his country abroad, which I was proud to hear of, what were we the better for that at home? The agent was one of your middlemen, who grind the face of the poor, and can never bear a man with a hat upon his head: he ferreted the tenants out of their lives; not a week without a call for money, drafts upon drafts from Sir Kit; but I laid it all to the fault of the agent; for, says I, what can Sir Kit do with so much cash, and he a single man?

[MIDDLEMEN.—There was a class of men, termed middlemen, in Ireland, who took large farms on long leases from gentlemen of landed property, and let the land again in small portions to the poor, as under-tenants, at exorbitant rents. The HEAD LANDLORD, as he was called, seldom saw his UNDER-TENANTS; but if he could not get the MIDDLEMAN to pay him his rent punctually, he WENT TO HIS LAND, AND

DROVE THE LAND FOR HIS RENT; that is to say, he sent his steward, or bailiff, or driver, to the land to seize the cattle, hay, corn, flax, oats, or potatoes, belonging to the under-tenants, and proceeded to sell these for his rents. It sometimes happened that these unfortunate tenants paid their rent twice over, once to the MIDDLEMAN, and once to the HEAD LANDLORD.

The characteristics of a middleman were servility to his superiors and tyranny towards his inferiors: the poor detested this race of beings. In speaking to them, however, they always used the most abject language, and the most humble tone and posture—'PLEASE YOUR HONOUR; AND PLEASE YOUR HONOUR'S HONOUR,' they knew must be repeated as a charm at the beginning and end of every equivocating, exculpatory, or supplicatory sentence; and they were much more alert in doffing their caps to those new men than to those of what they call GOOD OLD FAMILIES. A witty carpenter once termed these middlemen JOURNEYMEN GENTLEMEN.]

But still it went. Rents must be all paid up to the day, and afore; no allowance for improving tenants, no consideration for those who had built upon their farms: no sooner was a lease out, but the land was advertised to the highest bidder; all the old tenants turned out, when they spent their substance in the hope and trust of a renewal from the landlord. All was now let at the highest penny to a parcel of poor wretches, who meant to run away, and did so, after taking two crops out of the ground. Then fining down the year's rent came into fashion [GLOSSARY 16]—anything for the ready penny; and with all this and presents to the agent and the driver [GLOSSARY 17], there was no such thing as standing it. I said nothing, for I had a regard for the family; but I walked about thinking if his honour Sir Kit knew all this, it would go hard with him but he'd see us righted; not that I had anything for my own share to complain of, for the agent was always very civil to me when he came down into the country, and took a great deal of notice of my son Jason. Jason Quirk, though he be my son, I must say was a good scholar from his birth, and a very 'cute lad: I thought to make him a priest [GLOSSARY 18], but he did better for himself; seeing how he was as good a clerk as any in the county, the agent gave him his rent accounts to copy, which he did first of all for the pleasure of obliging the gentleman, and would take nothing at all for his trouble, but was always proud to serve the family. By and by a good farm bounding us to the east fell into his honour's hands, and my son put in a proposal for it: why shouldn't he, as well as another? The proposals all went over to the master at the Bath, who knowing no more of the land than the child unborn, only having once been out a-grousing on it before he went to England; and the value of lands, as the agent informed him, falling every year in Ireland, his honour wrote over in all haste a bit of a letter, saying he left it all to the agent, and that he must let it as well as he could—to the best bidder, to be sure—and send him over L200 by return of post: with this the agent gave me a hint, and I spoke a good word for my son, and gave out in the country that nobody need bid against us. So his proposal was just the thing, and he a good tenant; and he got a promise of an abatement in the rent after the first year, for advancing the half-year's rent at signing the lease, which was wanting to complete the agent's L200 by the return of the post, with all which my master wrote back he was well satisfied. About this time we learnt from the agent, as a great secret, how the money went so fast, and the reason of the thick coming of the master's drafts: he was a little too fond of play; and Bath, they say, was no place for no young man of his fortune, where there were so many of his own countrymen, too, hunting him up and down, day and night, who had nothing to lose. At last, at Christmas, the agent wrote over to stop the drafts, for he could raise no more money on bond or mortgage, or from the tenants, or anyhow, nor had he any more to lend himself, and desired at the same time to decline the agency for the future, wishing Sir Kit his health and happiness, and the compliments of the season, for I saw the letter before ever it was sealed, when my son copied it. When the answer came there was a new turn in affairs, and the agent was turned out; and my son Jason, who had corresponded privately with his honour occasionally on business, was forthwith desired by his honour to take the accounts into his own hands, and look them over, till further orders. It was a very spirited letter to be sure: Sir Kit sent his service, and the compliments of the season, in return to the agent, and he would fight him with pleasure to-morrow, or any day, for sending him such a letter, if he was born a gentleman, which he was sorry (for both their sakes) to find (too late) he was not. Then, in a private postscript, he condescended to tell us that all would be speedily settled to his satisfaction, and we should turn over a new leaf, for he was going to be married in a fortnight to the grandest heiress in England, and had only immediate occasion at present for L200, as he would not choose to touch his lady's fortune for travelling expenses home to Castle Rackrent, where he intended to be, wind and weather permitting, early in the next month; and desired fires, and the house to be painted, and the new building to go on as fast as possible, for the reception of him and his lady before that time; with several words besides in the letter, which we could not make out because, God bless him! he wrote in such a flurry. My heart warmed to my new lady when I read this: I was almost afraid it was too good news to be true; but the girls fell to scouring, and it was well they did, for we soon saw his marriage in the paper, to a lady with I don't know how many tens of thousand pounds to her fortune: then I watched the post-office for his landing; and the news came to my son of his and the bride being in Dublin, and on the way home to Castle Rackrent. We had bonfires all over the country, expecting him down the next day, and we had his coming of age still to celebrate, which he had not time to do properly before he left the country; therefore, a great ball was expected, and great doings upon his coming, as it were, fresh to take possession of his ancestors' estate. I never shall forget the day he came home; we had waited and waited all day long till eleven o'clock at night, and I was thinking of sending the boy to lock the gates, and giving them up for that night, when there came the carriages thundering up to the great hall door. I got the first sight of the bride; for when the carriage door opened, just as she had her foot on the steps, I held the flam full in her face to light her [*GLOSSARY 19*], at which she shut her eyes, but I had a full view of the rest of her, and greatly shocked I was, for by that light she was little better than a blackamoor, and seemed crippled; but that was only sitting so long in the chariot.

'You're kindly welcome to Castle Rackrent, my lady,' says I (recollecting who she was). 'Did your honour hear of the bonfires?'

His honour spoke never a word, nor so much as handed her up the steps—he looked to me no more like himself than nothing at all; I know I took him for the skeleton of his honour. I was not sure what to say next to one or t'other, but seeing she was a stranger in a foreign country, I thought it but right to speak cheerful to her; so I went back again to the bonfires.

'My lady,' says I, as she crossed the hall, 'there would have been fifty times as many; but for fear of the horses, and frightening your ladyship, Jason and I forbid them, please your honour.'

With that she looked at me a little bewildered.

'Will I have a fire lighted in the state-room to-night?' was the next question I put to her, but never a word she answered; so I concluded she could not speak a word of English, and was from foreign parts. The short and the long of it was, I couldn't tell what to make of her; so I left her to herself, and went straight down to the servants' hall to learn something for certain about her. Sir Kit's own man was tired, but the groom set him a-talking at last, and we had it all out before ever I closed my eyes that night. The bride might well be a great fortune—she was a JEWISH by all accounts, who are famous for their great riches. I had never seen any of that tribe or nation before, and could only gather that she spoke a strange kind of English of her own, that she could not abide pork or sausages, and went neither to church or mass. Mercy upon his honour's poor soul, thought I; what will become of him and his, and all of us, with his heretic blackamoor at the head of the Castle Rackrent estate? I never slept a wink all night for thinking of it; but before the servants I put my pipe in my mouth, and kept my mind to myself, for I had a great regard for the family; and after this, when strange gentlemen's servants came to the house, and would begin to talk about the bride, I took care to put the best foot foremost, and passed her for a nabob in the kitchen, which accounted for her dark complexion and everything.

The very morning after they came home, however, I saw plain enough how things were between Sir Kit and my lady, though they were walking together arm in arm after breakfast, looking at the new building and the improvements.

'Old Thady,' said my master, just as he used to do, 'how do you do?'

'Very well, I thank your honour's honour,' said I; but I saw he was not well pleased, and my heart was in my mouth as I walked along after him.

'Is the large room damp, Thady?' said his honour.

'Oh damp, your honour! how should it be but as dry as a bone,' says I, 'after all the fires we have kept in it day and night? It's the barrack-room your honour's talking on [GLOSSARY 20].'

'And what is a barrack-room, pray, my dear?' were the first words I ever heard out of my lady's lips.

'No matter, my dear,' said he, and went on talking to me, ashamed-like I should witness her ignorance. To be sure, to hear her talk one might have taken her for an innocent [GLOSSARY 21], for it was, 'What's this, Sir Kit? and what's that, Sir Kit?' all the way we went. To be sure, Sir Kit had enough to do to answer her.

'And what do you call that, Sir Kit?' said she; 'that—that looks like a pile of black bricks, pray, Sir Kit?'

'My turf-stack, my dear,' said my master, and bit his lip.

Where have you lived, my lady, all your life, not to know a turf-stack when you see it? thought I; but I said nothing. Then by and by she takes out her glass, and begins spying over the country.

'And what's all that black swamp out yonder, Sir Kit?' says she.

'My bog, my dear,' says he, and went on whistling.

'It's a very ugly prospect, my dear,' says she.

'You don't see it, my dear,' says he, 'for we've planted it out; when the trees grow up in summer-time—' says he.

'Where are the trees,' said she, 'my dear?' still looking through her glass.

'You are blind, my dear,' says he; 'what are these under your eyes?'

'These shrubs?' said she.

'Trees,' said he.

'Maybe they are what you call trees in Ireland, my dear,' said she; 'but they are not a yard high, are they?'

'They were planted out but last year, my lady,' says I, to soften matters between them, for I saw she was going the way to make his honour mad with her: 'they are very well grown for their age, and you'll not see the bog of Allyballycarrick-o'shaughlin at-all-at-all through the skreen, when once the leaves come out. But, my lady, you must not quarrel with any part or parcel of Allyballycarricko'shaughlin, for you don't know how many hundred years that same bit of bog has been in the family; we would not part with the bog of Allyballycarricko'shaughlin upon no account at all; it cost the late Sir Murtagh two hundred good pounds to defend his title to it and boundaries against the O'Learys, who cut a road through it.'

Now one would have thought this would have been hint enough for my lady, but she fell to laughing like one out of their right mind, and made me say the name of the bog over, for her to get it by heart, a dozen times; then she must ask me how to spell it, and what was the meaning of it in English—Sir Kit standing by whistling all the while. I verily believed she laid the corner-stone of all her future misfortunes at that very instant; but I said no more, only looked at Sir Kit.

There were no balls, no dinners, no doings; the country was all disappointed—Sir Kit's gentleman said in a whisper to me, it was all my lady's own fault, because she was so obstinate about the cross.

'What cross?' says I; 'is it about her being a heretic?'

'Oh, no such matter,' says he; 'my master does not mind her heresies, but her diamond cross it's worth I can't tell you how much, and she has thousands of English pounds concealed in diamonds about her, which she as good as promised to give up to my master before he married; but now she won't part with any of them, and she must take the consequences.'

Her honeymoon, at least her Irish honeymoon, was scarcely well over, when his honour one morning said to me, 'Thady, buy me a pig!' and then the sausages were ordered, and here was the first open breaking-out of my lady's troubles. My lady came down herself into the kitchen to speak to the cook about the sausages, and desired never to see them more at her table. Now my master had ordered them, and my lady knew that. The cook took my lady's part, because she never came down into the kitchen, and was young and innocent in housekeeping, which raised her pity; besides, said she, at her own table, surely my lady should order and disorder what she pleases. But the cook soon changed her note, for my master made it a principle to have the sausages, and swore at her for a Jew herself, till he drove her fairly out of the kitchen; then, for fear of her place, and because he threatened that my lady should give her no discharge without the sausages, she gave up, and from that day forward always sausages, or bacon, or pig-meat in some shape or other, went up to table; upon which my lady shut herself up in her own room, and my master said she might stay there, with an oath: and to make sure of her, he turned the key in the door, and kept it ever after in his pocket. We none of us ever saw or heard her speak for seven years after that: he carried her dinner himself.

[This part of the history of the Rackrent family can scarcely be thought credible; but in justice to honest Thady, it is hoped the reader will recollect the history of the celebrated Lady Cathcart's conjugal imprisonment. The editor was acquainted with Colonel M'Guire, Lady Cathcart's husband; he has lately seen and questioned the maid-servant who lived with Colonel M'Guire during the time of Lady Cathcart's imprisonment. Her ladyship was locked up in her own house for many years, during which period her husband was visited by the neighbouring gentry, and it was his regular custom at dinner to send his compliments to Lady Cathcart, informing her that the company had the honour to drink her ladyship's health, and begging to know whether there was anything at table that she would like to eat? The answer was always, 'Lady Cathcart's compliments, and she has everything she wants.' An instance of honesty in a poor Irishwoman deserves to be recorded. Lady Cathcart had some remarkably fine diamonds, which she had concealed from her husband, and which she was anxious to get out of the house, lest he should discover them. She had neither servant nor friend to whom she could entrust them, but she had observed a poor beggar woman, who used to come to the house; she spoke to her from the window of the room in which she was confined; the woman promised to do what she desired, and Lady Cathcart threw a parcel containing the jewels to her. The poor woman carried them to the person to whom they were directed, and several years afterwards, when Lady Cathcart recovered her liberty, she received her diamonds safely.

At Colonel M'Guire's death her ladyship was released. The editor, within this year, saw the gentleman who accompanied her to England after her husband's death. When she first was told of his death she imagined that the news was not true, and that it was told only with an intention of deceiving her. At his death she had scarcely clothes sufficient to cover her; she wore a red wig, looked scared, and her understanding seemed stupefied; she said that she scarcely knew one human creature from another; her imprisonment lasted above twenty years. These circumstances may appear strange to an English reader; but there is no danger in the present times that any individual should exercise such tyranny as Colonel M'Guire's with impunity, the power being now all in the hands of Government, and there being no possibility of obtaining from Parliament an Act of indemnity for any cruelties.]

Then his honour had a great deal of company to dine with him, and balls in the house, and was as gay and gallant, and as much himself as before he was married; and at dinner he always drank my Lady Rackrent's good health and so did the company, and he sent out always a servant with his compliments to my Lady Rackrent, and the company was drinking her ladyship's health, and begged to know if there was anything at table he might send her, and the man came back, after the sham errand, with my Lady Rackrent's compliments, and she was very much obliged to Sir Kit—she did not wish for anything, but drank the company's health. The country, to be sure, talked and wondered at my lady's being shut up, but nobody chose to interfere or ask any impertinent questions, for they knew my master was a man very apt to give a short answer himself, and likely to call a man out for it afterwards: he was a famous shot, had killed his man before he came of age, and nobody scarce dared look at him whilst at Bath. Sir Kit's character was so well known in the country that he lived in peace and quietness ever after, and was a great favourite with the ladies, especially when in process of time, in the fifth year of her confinement, my Lady Rackrent fell ill and took entirely to her bed, and he gave out that she was now skin and bone, and could not last through the winter. In this he had two physicians' opinions to back him (for now he called in two physicians for her), and tried all his arts to get the diamond cross from her on her death-bed, and to get her to make a will in his favour of her separate possessions; but there she was too tough for him. He used to swear at her behind her back after kneeling to her face, and call her in the presence of his gentleman his stiff-necked Israelite, though before he married her that same gentleman told me he used to call her (how he could bring it out, I don't know) 'my pretty Jessica!' To be sure it must have been hard for her to guess what sort of a husband he reckoned to make her. When she was lying, to all expectation, on her death-bed of a broken heart, I could not but pity her, though she was a Jewish, and considering too it was no fault of hers to be taken with my master, so young as she was at the Bath, and so fine a gentleman as Sir Kit was when he courted her; and considering too, after all they had heard and seen of him as a husband, there were now no less than three ladies in our county talked of for his second wife, all at daggers drawn with each other, as his gentleman swore, at the balls, for Sir Kit for their partner—I could not but think them bewitched, but they all reasoned with themselves that Sir Kit would make a good husband to any Christian but a Jewish, I suppose, and especially as he was now a reformed rake; and it was not known how my lady's fortune was settled in her will, nor how the Castle Rackrent estate was all mortgaged, and bonds out against him, for he was never cured of his gaming tricks; but that was the only fault he had, God bless him!

My lady had a sort of fit, and it was given out that she was dead, by mistake: this brought things to a sad crisis for my poor master. One of the three ladies showed his letters to her brother, and claimed his promises, whilst another did the same. I don't mention names. Sir Kit, in his defence, said he would meet any man who dared to question his conduct; and as to the ladies, they must settle it amongst them who was to be his second, and his third, and his fourth, whilst his first was still alive, to his mortification and theirs. Upon this, as upon all former occasions, he had the voice of the country with him, on account of the great spirit and propriety he acted with. He met and shot the first lady's brother: the next day he called out the second, who had a wooden leg, and their place of meeting by appointment being in a new-ploughed field, the wooden-leg man stuck fast in it. Sir Kit, seeing his situation, with great candour fired his pistol over his head; upon which the seconds interposed, and convinced the parties there had been a slight misunderstanding between them: thereupon they shook hands cordially, and went home to dinner together. This gentleman, to show the world how they stood together, and by the advice of the friends of both parties, to re-establish his sister's injured reputation, went out with Sir Kit as his second, and carried his message next day to the last of his adversaries: I never saw him in such fine spirits as that day he went out—sure enough he was within ames-ace of getting quit handsomely of all his enemies; but unluckily, after hitting the toothpick out of his adversary's finger and thumb, he received a ball in a vital part, and was brought home, in little better than an hour after the affair, speechless on a hand-barrow to my lady. We got the key out of his pocket the first thing we did, and my son Jason ran to unlock the barrack-room, where my lady had been shut up for seven years, to acquaint her with the fatal accident. The surprise bereaved her of her senses at first, nor would she believe but we were putting some new trick upon her, to entrap her out of her jewels, for a great while, till Jason bethought himself of taking her to the window, and showed her the men bringing Sir Kit up the avenue upon the hand-barrow, which had immediately the desired effect; for directly she burst into tears, and pulling her cross from her bosom, she kissed it with as great devotion as ever I witnessed, and lifting up her eyes to heaven, uttered some ejaculation, which none present heard; but I take the sense of it to be, she returned thanks for this unexpected interposition in her favour when she had least reason to expect it. My master was greatly lamented: there was no life in him when we lifted him off the barrow, so he was laid out immediately, and 'waked' the same night. The country was all in an uproar about him, and not a soul but cried shame upon his murderer, who would have been hanged surely, if he could have been brought to his trial, whilst the gentlemen in the country were up about it; but he very prudently withdrew himself to the Continent before the affair was made public. As for the young lady who was the immediate cause of the fatal accident, however innocently, she could never show her head after at the balls in the county or any place; and by the advice of her friends and physicians, she was ordered soon after to Bath, where it was expected, if anywhere on this side of the grave, she would meet with the recovery of her health and lost peace of mind. As a proof of his great popularity, I need only add that there was a song made upon my master's untimely death in the newspapers, which was in everybody's mouth, singing up and down through the country, even down to the mountains, only three days after his unhappy exit. He was also greatly bemoaned at the Curragh [GLOSSARY 22], where his cattle were well known; and all who had taken up his bets were particularly inconsolable for his loss to society. His stud sold at the cant at the greatest price ever known in the county [GLOSSARY 23]; his favourite horses were chiefly disposed of amongst his particular friends, who would give any price for them for his sake; but no ready money was required by the new heir, who wished not to displease any of the gentlemen of the neighbourhood just upon his coming to settle amongst them; so a long credit was given where requisite, and the cash has never been gathered in from that day to this.

But to return to my lady. She got surprisingly well after my master's decease. No sooner was it known for certain that he was dead, than all the gentlemen within twenty miles of us came in a body, as it were, to set my lady at liberty, and to protest against her confinement, which they now for the first time understood was against her own consent. The ladies too were as attentive as possible, striving who should be foremost with their morning visits; and they that saw the diamonds spoke very handsomely of them, but thought it a pity they were not bestowed, if it had so pleased God, upon a lady who would have become them better. All these civilities wrought little with my lady, for she had taken an unaccountable prejudice against the country, and everything belonging to it, and was so partial to her native land, that after parting with the cook, which she did immediately upon my master's decease, I never knew her easy one instant, night or day, but when she was packing up to leave us. Had she meant to make any stay in Ireland, I stood a great chance of being a great favourite with her; for when she found I understood the weathercock, she was always finding some pretence to be talking to me, and asking me which way the wind blew, and was it likely, did I think, to continue fair for England. But when I saw she had made up her mind to spend the rest of her days upon her own income and jewels in England, I considered her quite as a foreigner, and not at all any longer as part of the family. She gave no vails to the servants at Castle Rackrent at parting, notwithstanding the old proverb of 'as rich as a Jew,' which she, being a Jewish, they built upon with reason. But from first to last she brought nothing but misfortunes amongst us; and if it had not been all along with her, his honour, Sir Kit, would have been now alive in all appearance. Her diamond cross was, they say, at the bottom of it all; and it was a shame for her, being his wife, not to show more duty, and to have given it up when he condescended to ask so often for such a bit of a trifle in his distresses, especially when he all along made it no secret he married for money. But we will not bestow another thought upon her. This much I thought it lay upon my conscience to say, in justice to my poor master's memory.

'Tis an ill wind that blows nobody no good: the same wind that took the Jew Lady Rackrent over to England brought over the new heir to Castle Rackrent.

Here let me pause for breath in my story, for though I had a great regard for every member of the family, yet without compare Sir Conolly, commonly called, for short, amongst his friends, Sir Condy Rackrent, was ever my great favourite, and, indeed, the most universally beloved man I had ever seen or heard of, not excepting his great ancestor Sir Patrick, to whose memory he, amongst other instances of generosity, erected a handsome marble stone in the church of Castle Rackrent, setting forth in large letters his age, birth, parentage, and many other virtues, concluding with the compliment so justly due, that 'Sir Patrick Rackrent lived and died a monument of old Irish hospitality.'

CONTINUATION OF THE MEMOIRS OF THE RACKRENT FAMILY

HISTORY OF SIR CONOLLY RACKRENT

Sir Condy Rackrent, by the grace of God heir-at-law to the Castle Rackrent estate, was a remote branch of the family. Born to little or no fortune of his own, he was bred to the bar, at which, having many friends to push him and no mean natural abilities of his own, he doubtless would in process of time, if he could have borne the drudgery of that study, have been rapidly made King's Counsel at the least; but things were disposed of otherwise, and he never went the circuit but twice, and then made no figure for want of a fee, and being unable to speak in public. He received his education chiefly in the college of Dublin, but before he came to years of discretion lived in the country, in a small but slated house within view of the end of the avenue. I remember him, bare footed and headed, running through the street of O'Shaughlin's Town, and playing at pitch-and-toss, ball, marbles, and what not, with the boys of the town, amongst whom my son Jason was a great favourite with him. As for me, he was ever my white-headed boy: often's the time, when I would call in at his father's, where I was always made welcome, he would slip down to me in the kitchen, and, love to sit on my knee whilst I told him stories of the family and the blood from which he was sprung, and how he might look forward, if the then present man should die without childer, to being at the head of the Castle Rackrent estate. This was then spoke quite and clear at random to please the child, but it pleased Heaven to accomplish my prophecy afterwards, which gave him a great opinion of my judgment in business. He went to a little grammar-school with many others, and my son amongst the rest, who was in his class, and not a little useful to him in his book-learning, which he acknowledged with gratitude ever after. These rudiments of his education thus completed, he got a-horseback, to which exercise he was ever addicted, and used to gallop over the country while yet but a slip of a boy, under the care of Sir Kit's huntsman, who was very fond of him, and often lent him his gun, and took him out a-shooting under his own eye. By these means he became well acquainted and popular amongst the poor in the neighbourhood early, for there was not a cabin at which he had not stopped some morning or other, along with the huntsman, to drink a glass of burnt whisky out of an eggshell, to do him good and warm his heart and drive the cold out of his stomach. The old people always told him he was a great likeness of Sir Patrick, which made him first have an ambition to take after him, as far as his fortune should allow. He left us when of an age to enter the college, and there completed his education and nineteenth year, for as he was not born to an estate, his friends thought it incumbent on them to give him the best education which could be had for love or money, and a great deal of money consequently was spent upon him at College and Temple. He was a very little altered for the worse by what he saw there of the great world, for when he came down into the country to pay us a visit, we thought him just the same man as ever—hand and glove with every one, and as far from high, though not without his own proper share of family pride, as any man ever you see. Latterly, seeing how Sir Kit and the Jewish lived together, and that there was no one between him and the Castle Rackrent estate, he neglected to apply to the law as much as was expected of him, and secretly many of the tenants and others advanced him cash upon his note of hand value received, promising bargains of leases and lawful interest, should he ever come into the estate. All this was kept a great secret for fear the present man, hearing of it, should take it into his head to take it ill of poor Condy, and so should cut him off for ever by levying a fine, and suffering a recovery to dock the entail [*GLOSSARY 24*]. Sir Murtagh would have been the man for that; but Sir Kit was too much taken up philandering to consider the law in this case, or any other. These practices I have mentioned to account for the state of his affairs—I mean Sir Condy's upon his coming into the Castle Rackrent estate. He could not command a penny of his first year's income, which, and keeping no accounts, and the great sight of company he did, with many other causes too numerous to mention, was the origin of his distresses. My son Jason, who was now established agent, and knew everything, explained matters out of the face to Sir Conolly, and made him sensible of his embarrassed situation. With a great nominal rent-roll, it was almost all paid away in interest; which being for convenience suffered to run on, soon doubled the principal, and Sir Condy was obliged to pass new bonds for the interest, now grown principal, and so on. Whilst this was going on, my son requiring to be paid for his trouble and many years' service in the family gratis, and Sir Condy not willing to take his affairs into his own hands, or to look them even in the face, he gave my son a bargain of some acres which fell out of lease at a reasonable rent. Jason set the land, as soon as his lease was sealed, to under-tenants, to make the rent, and got two hundred a year profit rent; which was little enough considering his long agency. He bought the land at twelve years' purchase two years afterwards, when Sir Condy was pushed for money on an execution, and was at the same time allowed for his improvements thereon. There was a sort of hunting-lodge upon the estate, convenient to my son Jason's land, which he had his eye upon about this time; and he was a little jealous of Sir Condy, who talked of setting it to a stranger who was just come into the country—Captain Moneygawl was the man. He was son and heir to the Moneygawls of Mount Juliet's Town, who had a great estate in the next county to ours; and my master was loth to disoblige the young gentleman, whose heart was set upon the Lodge; so he wrote him back that the Lodge was at his service, and if he would honour him with his company at Castle Rackrent, they could ride over together some morning and look at it before signing the lease. Accordingly, the captain came over to us, and he and Sir Condy grew the greatest friends ever you see, and were for ever out a-shooting or hunting together, and were very merry in the evenings; and Sir Condy was invited of course to Mount Juliet's Town; and the family intimacy that had been in Sir Patrick's time was now recollected, and nothing would serve Sir Condy but he must be three times a week at the least with his new friends, which grieved me, who knew, by the captain's groom and gentleman, how they talked of him at Mount Juliet's Town, making him quite, as one may say, a laughing-stock and a butt for the whole company; but they were soon cured of that by an accident that surprised 'em not a little, as it did me. There was a bit of a scrawl found upon the waiting-maid of old Mr. Moneygawl's youngest daughter, Miss Isabella, that laid open the whole; and her father, they say, was like one out of his right mind, and swore it was the last thing he ever should have thought of, when he invited my master to his house, that his daughter should think of such a match. But their talk signified not a straw, for as Miss Isabella's maid reported, her young mistress was fallen over head and ears in love with Sir Condy from the first time that ever her brother brought him into the house to dinner. The servant who waited that day behind my master's chair was the first who knew it, as he says; though it's hard to believe him, for he did not tell it till a great while afterwards; but, however, it's likely enough, as the thing turned out, that he was not far out of the way, for towards the middle of dinner, as he says, they were talking of stage-plays, having a playhouse, and being great play-actors at Mount Juliet's Town; and Miss Isabella turns short to my master, and says:

'Have you seen the play-bill, Sir Condy?'

'No, I have not,' said he.

'Then more shame for you,' said the captain her brother, 'not to know that my sister is to play Juliet to-night, who plays it better than any woman on or off the stage in all Ireland.'

'I am very happy to hear it,' said Sir Condy; and there the matter dropped for the present.

But Sir Condy all this time, and a great while afterwards, was at a terrible nonplus; for he had no liking, not he, to stage-plays, nor to Miss Isabella either—to his mind, as it came out over a bowl of whisky-punch at home, his little Judy M'Quirk, who was daughter to a sister's son of mine, was worth twenty of Miss Isabella. He had seen her often when he stopped at her father's cabin to drink whisky out of the eggshell, out hunting, before he came to the estate, and, as she gave out, was under something like a promise of marriage to her. Anyhow, I could not but pity my poor master, who was so bothered between them, and he an easy-hearted man, that could not disoblige nobody—God bless him! To be sure, it was not his place to behave ungenerous to Miss Isabella, who had disobliged all her relations for his sake, as he remarked; and then she was locked up in her chamber, and forbid to think of him any more, which raised his spirit, because his family was, as he observed, as good as theirs at any rate, and the Rackrents a suitable match for the Moneygawls any day in the year; all which was true enough. But it grieved me to see that, upon the strength of all this, Sir Condy was growing more in the mind to carry off Miss Isabella to Scotland, in spite of her relations, as she desired.

'It's all over with our poor Judy!' said I, with a heavy sigh, making bold to speak to him one night when he was a little cheerful, and standing in the servants' hall all alone with me as was often his custom.

'Not at all,' said he; 'I never was fonder of Judy than at this present speaking; and to prove it to you,' said he—and he took from my hand a halfpenny change that I had just got along with my tobacco—'and to prove it to you, Thady,' says he, 'it's a toss-up with me which I should marry this minute, her or Mr. Moneygawl of Mount Juliet's Town's daughter—so it is.'

Oh-boo! boo!' [Boo! Boo!—an exclamation equivalent to PSHAW or NONSENSE] says I, making light of it, to see what he would go on to next; 'your honour's joking, to be sure; there's no compare between our poor Judy and Miss Isabella, who has a great fortune, they say.'

'I'm not a man to mind a fortune, nor never was,' said Sir Condy, proudly, 'whatever her friends may say; and to make short of it,' says he, 'I'm come to a determination upon the spot.' With that he swore such a terrible oath as made me cross myself. 'And by this book,' said he, snatching up my ballad-book, mistaking it for my prayer-book, which lay in the window,—'and by this book,' says he, 'and by all the books that ever were shut and opened, it's come to a toss-up with me, and I'll stand or fall by the toss; and so Thady, hand me over that pin [PIN, read PEN.—It formerly was vulgarly pronounced PIN in Ireland] out of the ink-horn;' and he makes a cross on the smooth side of the halfpenny; 'Judy M'Quirk,' says he, 'her mark.'

[HER MARK.—It was the custom in Ireland for those who could not write to make a cross to stand for their signature, as was formerly the practice of our English monarchs. The Editor inserts the facsimile of an Irish mark, which may hereafter be valuable to a judicious antiquary—

Her
Judy X M'Quirk,
Mark.

In bonds or notes signed in this manner a witness is requisite, as the name is frequently written by him or her.]

God bless him! his hand was a little unsteadied by all the whisky-punch he had taken, but it was plain to see his heart was for poor Judy. My heart was all as one as in my mouth when I saw the halfpenny up in the air, but I said nothing at all; and when it came down I was glad I had kept myself to myself, for to be sure now it was all over with poor Judy.

'Judy's out a luck,' said I, striving to laugh.

'I'm out a luck,' said he; and I never saw a man look so cast down: he took up the halfpenny off the flag, and walked away quite sober-like by the shock. Now, though as easy a man, you would think, as any in the wide world, there was no such thing as making him unsay one of these sort of vows, which he had learned to reverence when young, as I well remember teaching him to toss up for bog-berries on my knee. [VOWS.—It has been maliciously and unjustly hinted that the lower classes of the people of Ireland pay but little regard to oaths; yet it is certain that some oaths or vows have great power over their minds. Sometimes they swear they will be revenged on some of their neighbours; this is an oath that they are never known to break. But, what is infinitely more extraordinary and unaccountable, they sometimes make and keep a vow against whisky; these vows are usually limited to a short time. A woman who has a drunken husband is most fortunate if she can prevail upon him to go to the priest, and make a vow against whisky for a year, or a month, or a week, or a day.] So I saw the affair was as good as settled between him and Miss Isabella, and I had no more to say but to wish her joy, which I did the week afterwards, upon her return from Scotland with my poor master.

My new lady was young, as might be supposed of a lady that had been carried off by her own consent to Scotland; but I could only see her at first through her veil, which, from bashfulness or fashion, she kept over her face.

'And am I to walk through all this crowd of people, my dearest love?' said she to Sir Condy, meaning us servants and tenants, who had gathered at the back gate.

'My dear,' said Sir Condy, 'there's nothing for it but to walk, or to let me carry you as far as the house, for you see the back road is too narrow for a carriage, and the great piers have tumbled down across the front approach; so there's no driving the right way, by reason of the ruins.'

'Plato, thou reasonest well!' said she, or words to that effect, which I could noways understand; and again, when her foot stumbled against a broken bit of a car-wheel, she cried out, 'Angels and ministers of grace defend us!' Well, thought I, to be sure, if she's no Jewish, like the last, she is a mad woman for certain, which is as bad: it would have been as well for my poor master to have taken up with poor Judy, who is in her right mind anyhow.

She was dressed like a mad woman, moreover, more than like any one I ever saw afore or since, and I could not take my eyes off her, but still followed behind her; and her feathers on the top of her hat were broke going in at the low back door and she pulled out her little bottle out of her pocket to smell when she found herself in the kitchen, and said, 'I shall faint with the heat of this odious, odious place.'

'My dear, it's only three steps across the kitchen, and there's a fine air if your veil was up,' said Sir Condy; and with that threw back her veil, so that I had then a full sight of her face. She had not at all the colour of one going to faint, but a fine complexion of her own, as I then took it to be, though her maid told me after it was all put on; but even, complexion and all taken in, she was no way, in point of good looks, to compare to poor Judy, and withal she had a quality toss with her; but maybe it was my over-partiality to Judy, into whose place I may say she stepped, that made me notice all this.

To do her justice, however, she was, when we came to know her better, very liberal in her housekeeping—nothing at all of the skinflint in her; she left everything to the housekeeper, and her own maid, Mrs. Jane, who went with her to Scotland, gave her the best of characters for generosity. She seldom or ever wore a thing twice the same way, Mrs. Jane told us, and was always pulling her things to pieces and giving them away, never being used, in her father's house, to think of expense in anything; and she reckoned to be sure to go on the same way at Castle Rackrent; but when I came to inquire, I learned that her father was so mad with her for running off, after his locking her up and forbidding her to think any more of Sir Condy, that he would not give her a farthing; and it was lucky for her she had a few thousands of her own, which had been left to her by a good grandmother, and these were very convenient to begin with. My master and my lady set out in great style; they had the finest coach and chariot, and horses and liveries, and cut the greatest dash in the county, returning their wedding visits; and it was immediately reported that her father had undertaken to pay all my master's debts, and of course all his tradesmen gave him a new credit, and everything went on smack smooth, and I could not but admire my lady's spirit, and was proud to see Castle Rackrent again in all its glory. My lady had a fine taste for building, and furniture, and playhouses, and she turned everything topsy-turvy, and made the barrack-room into a theatre, as she called it, and she went on as if she had a mint of money at her elbow; and to be sure I thought she knew best, especially as Sir Condy said nothing to it one way or the other. All he asked—God bless him!—was to live in peace and quietness, and have his bottle or his whisky-punch at night to himself. Now this was little enough, to be sure, for any gentleman; but my lady couldn't abide the smell of the whisky-punch.

'My dear,' says he, 'you liked it well enough before we were married, and why not now?'

'My dear,' said she, 'I never smelt it, or I assure you I should never have prevailed upon myself to marry you.'

'My dear, I am sorry you did not smell it, but we can't help that now,' returned my master, without putting himself in a passion, or going out of his way, but just fair and easy helped himself to another glass, and drank it off to her good health.

All this the butler told me, who was going backwards and forwards unnoticed with the jug, and hot water, and sugar, and all he thought wanting. Upon my master's swallowing the last glass of whisky-punch my lady burst into tears, calling him an ungrateful, base, barbarous wretch; and went off into a fit of hysterics, as I think Mrs. Jane called it, and my poor master was greatly frightened, this being the first thing of the kind he had seen; and he fell straight on his knees before her, and, like a good-hearted cratur as he was, ordered the whisky-punch out of the room, and bid 'em throw open all the windows, and cursed himself: and then my lady came to herself again, and when she saw him kneeling there, bid him get up, and not forswear himself any more, for that she was sure he did not love her, and never had. This we learned from Mrs. Jane, who was the only person left present at all this.

'My dear,' returns my master, thinking, to be sure, of Judy, as well he might, 'whoever told you so is an incendiary, and I'll have 'em turned out of the house this minute, if you'll only let me know which of them it was.'

'Told me what?' said my lady, starting upright in her chair.

'Nothing at all, nothing at all,' said my master, seeing he had overshot himself, and that my lady spoke at random; 'but what you said just now, that I did not love you, Bella; who told you that?'

'My own sense,' she said, and she put her handkerchief to her face, and leant back upon Mrs. Jane, and fell to sobbing as if her heart would break.

'Why now, Bella, this is very strange of you,' said my poor master; 'if nobody has told you nothing, what is it you are taking on for at this rate, and exposing yourself and me for this way?'

'Oh, say no more, say no more; every word you say kills me,' cried my lady; and she ran on like one, as Mrs. Jane says, raving, 'Oh, Sir Condy, Sir Condy! I that had hoped to find in you—'

'Why now, faith, this is a little too much; do, Bella, try to recollect yourself, my dear; am not I your husband, and of your own choosing, and is not that enough?'

'Oh, too much! too much!' cried my lady, wringing her hands.

'Why, my dear, come to your right senses, for the love of heaven. See, is not the whisky-punch, jug and bowl and all, gone out of the room long ago? What is it, in the wide world, you have to complain of?'

But still my lady sobbed and sobbed, and called herself the most wretched of women; and among other out-of-the-way provoking things, asked my master, was he fit company for her, and he drinking all night? This nettling him, which it was hard to do, he replied, that as to drinking all night, he was then as sober as she was herself, and that it was no matter how much a man drank, provided it did noways affect or stagger him: that as to being fit company for her, he thought himself of a family to be fit company for any lord or lady in the land; but that he never prevented her from seeing and keeping what company she pleased, and that he had done his best to make Castle Rackrent pleasing to her since her marriage, having always had the house full of visitors, and if her own relations were not amongst them, he said that was their own fault, and their pride's fault, of which he was sorry to find her ladyship had so unbecoming a share. So concluding, he took his candle and walked off to his room, and my lady was in her tantarums for three days after; and would have been so much longer, no doubt, but some of her friends, young ladies, and cousins, and second cousins, came to Castle Rackrent, by my poor master's express invitation, to see her, and she was in a hurry to get up, as Mrs. Jane called it, a play for them, and so got well, and was as finely dressed, and as happy to look at, as ever; and all the young ladies, who used to be in her room dressing of her, said in Mrs. Jane's hearing that my lady was the happiest bride ever they had seen, and that to be sure a love-match was the only thing for happiness, where the parties could any way afford it.

As to affording it, God knows it was little they knew of the matter; my lady's few thousands could not last for ever, especially the way she went on with them; and letters from tradesfolk came every post thick and threefold, with bills as long as my arm, of years' and years' standing. My son Jason had 'em all handed over to him, and the pressing letters were all unread by Sir Condy, who hated trouble, and could never be brought to hear talk of business, but still put it off and put it off, saying, 'Settle it anyhow,' or, 'Bid 'em call again to-morrow,' or, 'Speak to me about it some other time.' Now it was hard to find the right time to speak, for in the mornings he was a-bed, and in the evenings over his bottle, where no gentleman chooses to be disturbed. Things in a twelvemonth or so came to such a pass there was no making a shift to go on any longer, though we were all of us well enough used to live from hand to mouth at Castle Rackrent. One day, I remember, when there was a power of company, all sitting after dinner in the dusk, not to say dark, in the drawing-room, my lady having rung five times for candles, and none to go up, the housekeeper sent up the footman, who went to my mistress, and whispered behind her chair how it was.

'My lady,' says he, 'there are no candles in the house.'

'Bless me,' says she; 'then take a horse and gallop off as fast as you can to Carrick O'Fungus, and get some.'

'And in the meantime tell them to step into the playhouse, and try if there are not some bits left,' added Sir Condy, who happened, to be within hearing. The man was sent up again to my lady, to let her know there was no horse to go, but one that wanted a shoe.

'Go to Sir Condy then; I know nothing at all about the horses,' said my lady; 'why do you plague me with these things?' How it was settled I really forget, but to the best of my remembrance, the boy was sent down to my son Jason's to borrow candles for the night. Another time, in the winter, and on a desperate cold day, there was no turf in for the parlour and above stairs, and scarce enough for the cook in the kitchen. The little GOSSOON was sent off to the neighbours, to see and beg or borrow some, but none could he bring back with him for love or money; [GOSSOON: a little boy—from the French word GARCON. In most Irish families there used to be a barefooted gossoon, who was slave to the cook and the butler, and who, in fact, without wages, did all the hard work of the house. Gossoons were always employed as messengers. The Editor has known a gossoon to go on foot, without shoes or stockings, fifty-one English miles between sunrise and sunset.] so, as needs must, we were forced to trouble Sir Condy—'Well, and if there's no turf to be had in the town or country, why, what signifies talking any more about it; can't ye go and cut down a tree?'

'Which tree, please your honour?' I made bold to say.

'Any tree at all that's good to burn,' said Sir Condy; 'send off smart and get one down, and the fires lighted, before my lady gets up to breakfast, or the house will be too hot to hold us.'

He was always very considerate in all things about my lady, and she wanted for nothing whilst he had it to give. Well, when things were tight with them about this time, my son Jason put in a word again about the Lodge, and made a genteel offer to lay down the purchase-money, to relieve Sir Condy's distresses. Now Sir Condy had it from the best authority that there were two writs come down to the sheriff against his person, and the sheriff, as ill-luck would have it, was no friend of his, and talked how he must do his duty, and how he would do it, if it was against the first man in the country, or even his own brother, let alone one who had voted against him at the last election, as Sir Condy had done. So Sir Condy was fain to take the purchase-money of the Lodge from my son Jason to settle matters; and sure enough it was a good bargain for both parties, for my son bought the fee-simple of a good house for him and his heirs for ever, for little or nothing, and by selling of it for that same my master saved himself from a gaol. Every way it turned out fortunate for Sir Condy, for before the money was all gone there came a general election, and he being so well beloved in the county, and one of the oldest families, no one had a better right to stand candidate for the vacancy; and he was called upon by all his friends, and the whole county I may say, to declare himself against the old member, who had little thought of a contest. My master did not relish the thoughts of a troublesome canvass, and all the ill-will he might bring upon himself by disturbing the peace of the county, besides the expense, which was no trifle; but all his friends called upon one another to subscribe, and they formed themselves into a committee, and wrote all his circular letters for him, and engaged all his agents, and did all the business unknown to him; and he was well pleased that it should be so at last, and my lady herself was very sanguine about the election; and there was open house kept night and day at Castle Rackrent, and I thought I never saw my lady look so well in her life as she did at that time. There were grand dinners, and all the gentlemen drinking success to Sir Condy till they were carried off; and then dances and balls, and the ladies all finishing with a raking pot of tea in the morning [GLOSSARY 25]. Indeed, it was well the company made it their choice to sit up all nights, for there were not half beds enough for the sights of people that were in it, though there were shake-downs in the drawing-room always made up before sunrise for those that liked it. For my part, when I saw the doings that were going on, and the loads of claret that went down the throats of them that had no right to be asking for it, and the sights of meat that went up to table and never came down, besides what was carried off to one or t'other below stair, I couldn't but pity my poor master, who was to pay for all; but I said nothing, for fear of gaining myself ill-will. The day of election will come some time or other, says I to myself, and all will be over; and so it did, and a glorious day it was as any I ever had the happiness to see.

'Huzza! huzza! Sir Condy Rackrent for ever!' was the first thing I hears in the morning, and the same and nothing else all day, and not a soul sober only just when polling, enough to give their votes as became 'em, and to stand the browbeating of the lawyers, who came tight enough upon us; and many of our freeholders were knocked off; having never a freehold that they could safely swear to, and Sir Condy was not willing to have any man perjure himself for his sake, as was done on the other side, God knows; but no matter for that. Some of our friends were dumbfounded by the lawyers asking them: Had they ever been upon the ground where their freeholds lay? Now, Sir Condy being tender of the consciences of them that had not been on the ground, and so could not swear to a freehold when cross-examined by them lawyers, sent out for a couple of cleavesful of the sods of his farm of Gulteeshinnagh; [At St. Patrick's meeting, London, March 1806, the Duke of Sussex said he had the honour of bearing an Irish title, and, with the permission of the company, he should tell them an anecdote of what he had experienced on his travels. When he was at Rome he went to visit an Irish seminary, and when they heard who it was, and that he had an Irish title, some of them asked him, 'Please your Royal Highness, since you are an Irish peer, will you tell us if you ever trod upon Irish ground?' When he told them he had not, 'Oh, then,' said one of the Order, 'you shall soon do so.' They then spread some earth, which had been brought from Ireland, on a marble slab, and made him stand upon it.] and as soon as the sods came into town, he set each man upon his sod, and so then, ever after, you know, they could fairly swear they had been upon the ground. [This was actually done at an election in Ireland.] We gained the day by this piece of honesty [*GLOSSARY 26*]. I thought I should have died in the streets for joy when I seed my poor master chaired, and he bareheaded, and it raining as hard as it could pour; but all the crowds following him up and down, and he bowing and shaking hands with the whole town.

'Is that Sir Condy Rackrent in the chair?' says a stranger man in the crowd.

'The same,' says I. 'Who else should it be? God bless him!'

'And I take it, then, you belong to him?' says he.

'Not at all,' says I; 'but I live under him, and have done so these two hundred years and upwards, me and mine.'

'It's lucky for you, then,' rejoins he, 'that he is where he is; for was he anywhere else but in the chair, this minute he'd be in a worse place; for I was sent down on purpose to put him up, [TO PUT HIM UP: to put him in gaol] and here's my order for so doing in my pocket.'

It was a writ that villain the wine merchant had marked against my poor master for some hundreds of an old debt, which it was a shame to be talking of at such a time as this.

'Put it in your pocket again, and think no more of it anyways for seven years to come, my honest friend,' says I; 'he's a member of Parliament now, praised be God, and such as you can't touch him: and if you'll take a fool's advice, I'd have you keep out of the way this day, or you'll run a good chance of getting your deserts amongst my master's friends, unless you choose to drink his health like everybody else.'

'I've no objection to that in life,' said he. So we went into one of the public-houses kept open for my master; and we had a great deal of talk about this thing and that. 'And how is it,' says he, 'your master keeps on so well upon his legs? I heard say he was off Holantide twelvemonth past.'

'Never was better or heartier in his life,' said I.

'It's not that I'm after speaking of' said he; 'but there was a great report of his being ruined.'

'No matter,' says I, 'the sheriffs two years running were his particular friends, and the sub-sheriffs were both of them gentlemen, and were properly spoken to; and so the writs lay snug with them, and they, as I understand by my son Jason the custom in them cases is, returned the writs as they came to them to those that sent 'em much good may it do them!—with a word in Latin, that no such person as Sir Condy Rackrent, Bart., was to be found in those parts.'

'Oh, I understand all those ways better—no offence—than you,' says he, laughing, and at the same time filling his glass to my master's good health, which convinced me he was a warm friend in his heart after all, though appearances were a little suspicious or so at first. 'To be sure,' says he, still cutting his joke, 'when a man's over head and shoulders in debt, he may live the faster for it, and the better if he goes the right way about it; or else how is it so many live on so well, as we see every day, after they are ruined?'

'How is it,' says I, being a little merry at the time—'how is it but just as you see the ducks in the chicken-yard, just after their heads are cut off by the cook, running round and round faster than when alive?'

At which conceit he fell a-laughing, and remarked he had never had the happiness yet to see the chicken-yard at Castle Rackrent.

'It won't be long so, I hope,' says I; 'you'll be kindly welcome there, as everybody is made by my master: there is not a freer-spoken gentleman, or a better beloved, high or low, in all Ireland.'

And of what passed after this I'm not sensible, for we drank Sir Candy's good health and the downfall of his enemies till we could stand no longer ourselves. And little did I think at the time, or till long after, how I was harbouring my poor master's greatest of enemies myself. This fellow had the impudence, after coming to see the chicken-yard, to get me to introduce him to my son Jason; little more than the man that never was born did I guess at his meaning by this visit: he gets him a correct list fairly drawn out from my son Jason of all my master's debts, and goes straight round to the creditors and buys them all up, which he did easy enough, seeing the half of them never expected to see their money out of Sir Condy's hands. Then, when this base-minded limb of the law, as I afterwards detected him in being, grew to be sole creditor over all, he takes him out a custodiam on all the denominations and sub-denominations, and even carton and half-carton upon the estate [GLOSSARY 27]; and not content with that, must have an execution against the master's goods and down to the furniture, though little worth, of Castle Rackrent itself. But this is a part of my story I'm not come to yet, and it's bad to be forestalling: ill news flies fast enough all the world over.

To go back to the day of the election, which I never think of but with pleasure and tears of gratitude for those good times: after the election was quite and clean over, there comes shoals of people from all parts, claiming to have obliged my master with their votes, and putting him in mind of promises which he could never remember himself to have made: one was to have a freehold for each of his four sons; another was to have a renewal of a lease; another an abatement; one came to be paid ten guineas for a pair of silver buckles sold my master on the hustings, which turned out to be no better than copper gilt; another had a long bill for oats, the half of which never went into the granary to my certain knowledge, and the other half was not fit for the cattle to touch; but the bargain was made the week before the election, and the coach and saddle-horses were got into order for the day, besides a vote fairly got by them oats; so no more reasoning on that head. But then there was no end to them that were telling Sir Condy he had engaged to make their sons excisemen, or high constables, or the like; and as for them that had bills to give in for liquor, and beds, and straw, and ribands, and horses, and post-chaises for the gentlemen freeholders that came from all parts and other counties to vote for my master, and were not, to be sure, to be at any charges, there was no standing against all these; and, worse than all, the gentlemen of my master's committee, who managed all for him, and talked how they'd bring him in without costing him a penny, and subscribed by hundreds very genteelly, forgot to pay their subscriptions, and had laid out in agents' and lawyers' fees and secret service money to the Lord knows how much; and my master could never ask one of them for their subscription you are sensible, nor for the price of a fine horse he had sold one of them; so it all was left at his door. He could never, God bless him again! I say, bring himself to ask a gentleman for money, despising such sort of conversation himself; but others, who were not gentlemen born, behaved very uncivil in pressing him at this very time, and all he could do to content 'em all was to take himself out of the way as fast as possible to Dublin, where my lady had taken a house fitting for him as a member of Parliament, to attend his duty in there all the winter. I was very lonely when the whole family was gone, and all the things they had ordered to go, and forgot, sent after them by the car. There was then a great silence in Castle Rackrent, and I went moping from room to room, hearing the doors clap for want of right locks, and the wind through the broken windows, that the glazier never would come to mend, and the rain coming through the roof and best ceilings all over the house for want of the slater, whose bill was not paid, besides our having no slates or shingles for that part of the old building which was shingled and burnt when the chimney took fire, and had been open to the weather ever since. I took myself to the servants' hall in the evening to smoke my pipe as usual, but missed the bit of talk we used to have there sadly, and ever after was content to stay in the kitchen and boil my little potatoes, [MY LITTLE POTATOES.—Thady does not mean by this expression that his potatoes were less than other people's, or less than the usual size. LITTLE is here used only as an Italian diminutive, expressive of fondness.] and put up my bed there, and every post-day I looked in the newspaper, but no news of my master in the House; he never spoke good or bad, but, as the butler wrote down word to my son Jason, was very ill-used by the Government about a place that was promised him and never given, after his supporting them against his conscience very honourably, and being greatly abused for it, which hurt him greatly, he having the name of a great patriot in the country before. The house and living in Dublin too were not to be had for nothing, and my son Jason said, 'Sir Condy must soon be looking out for a new agent, for I've done my part, and can do no more. If my lady had the bank of Ireland to spend, it would go all in one winter, and Sir Condy would never gainsay her, though he does not care the rind of a lemon for her all the while.'

Now I could not bear to hear Jason giving out after this manner against the family, and twenty people standing by in the street. Ever since he had lived at the Lodge of his own he looked down, howsomever, upon poor old Thady, and was grown quite a great gentleman, and had none of his relations near him; no wonder he was no kinder to poor Sir Condy than to his own kith or kin. [KITH AND KIN: family or relations. KIN from KIND; KITH from we know not what.] In the spring it was the villain that got the list of the debts from him brought down the custodiam, Sir Condy still attending his duty in Parliament and I could scarcely believe my own old eyes, or the spectacles with which I read it, when I was shown my son Jason's name joined in the custodiam; but he told me it was only for form's sake, and to make things easier than if all the land was under the power of a total stranger. Well, I did not know what to think; it was hard to be talking ill of my own, and I could not but grieve for my poor master's fine estate, all torn by these vultures of the law; so I said nothing, but just looked on to see how it would all end.

It was not till the month of June that he and my lady came down to the country. My master was pleased to take me aside with him to the brewhouse that same evening, to complain to me of my son and other matters, in which he said he was confident I had neither art nor part; he said a great deal more to me, to whom he had been fond to talk ever since he was my white-headed boy before he came to the estate; and all that he said about poor Judy I can never forget, but scorn to repeat. He did not say an unkind word of my lady, but wondered, as well he might, her relations would do nothing for him or her, and they in all this great distress. He did not take anything long to heart, let it be as it would, and had no more malice or thought of the like in him than a child that can't speak; this night it was all out of his head before he went to his bed. He took his jug of whisky-punch—my lady was grown quite easy about the whisky-punch by this time, and so I did suppose all was going on right betwixt them till I learnt the truth through Mrs. Jane, who talked over the affairs to the housekeeper, and I within hearing. The night my master came home, thinking of nothing at all but just making merry, he drank his bumper toast 'to the deserts of that old curmudgeon my father-in-law, and all enemies at Mount Juliet's Town.' Now my lady was no longer in the mind she formerly was, and did noways relish hearing her own friends abused in her presence, she said.

'Then why don't they show themselves your friends' said my master, 'and oblige me with the loan of the money I condescended, by your advice, my dear, to ask? It's now three posts since I sent off my letter, desiring in the postscript a speedy answer by the return of the post, and no account at all from them yet.'

'I expect they'll write to ME next post,' says my lady, and that was all that passed then; but it was easy from this to guess there was a coolness betwixt them, and with good cause.

The next morning, being post-day, I sent off the gossoon early to the post-office, to see was there any letter likely to set matters to rights, and he brought back one with the proper postmark upon it, sure enough, and I had no time to examine or make any conjecture more about it, for into the servants' hall pops Mrs. Jane with a blue bandbox in her hand, quite entirely mad.

'Dear ma'am, and what's the matter?' says I.

'Matter enough,' says she; 'don't you see my bandbox is wet through, and my best bonnet here spoiled, besides my lady's, and all by the rain coming in through that gallery window that you might have got mended if you'd had any sense, Thady, all the time we were in town in the winter?'

'Sure, I could not get the glazier, ma'am,' says I.

'You might have stopped it up anyhow,' says she.

'So I, did, ma'am, to the best of my ability; one of the panes with the old pillow-case, and the other with a piece of the old stage green curtain. Sure I was as careful as possible all the time you were away, and not a drop of rain came in at that window of all the windows in the house, all winter, ma'am, when under my care; and now the family's come home, and it's summer-time, I never thought no more about it, to be sure; but dear, it's a pity to think of your bonnet, ma'am. But here's what will please you, ma'am—a letter from Mount Juliet's Town for my lady.

With that she snatches it from me without a word more, and runs up the back stairs to my mistress; I follows with a slate to make up the window. This window was in the long passage, or gallery, as my lady gave out orders to have it called, in the gallery leading to my master's bedchamber and hers. And when I went up with the slate, the door having no lock, and the bolt spoilt, was ajar after Mrs. Jane, and, as I was busy with the window, I heard all that was saying within.

'Well, what's in your letter, Bella, my dear?' says he: 'you're a long time spelling it over.'

'Won't you shave this morning, Sir Condy?' says she, and put the letter into her pocket.

'I shaved the day before yesterday,' said he, 'my dear, and that's not what I'm thinking of now; but anything to oblige you, and to have peace and quietness, my dear'—and presently I had a glimpse of him at the cracked glass over the chimney-piece, standing up shaving himself to please my lady. But she took no notice, but went on reading her book, and Mrs. Jane doing her hair behind.

'What is it you're reading there, my dear?—phoo, I've cut myself with this razor; the man's a cheat that sold it me, but I have not paid him for it yet. What is it you're reading there? Did you hear me asking you, my dear?'

'THE SORROWS OF WERTHER,' replies my lady, as well as I could hear.

'I think more of the sorrows of Sir Condy,' says my master, joking like. 'What news from Mount Juliet's Town?'

'No news,' says she, 'but the old story over again; my friends all reproaching me still for what I can't help now.'

'Is it for marrying me?' said my master, still shaving. 'What signifies, as you say, talking of that, when it can't be help'd now?'

With that she heaved a great sigh that I heard plain enough in the passage.

'And did not you use me basely, Sir Condy,' says she, 'not to tell me you were ruined before I married you?'

'Tell you, my dear!' said he. 'Did you ever ask me one word about it. And had not your friends enough of your own, that were telling you nothing else from morning to night, if you'd have listened to them slanders?'

'No slanders, nor are my friends slanderers; and I can't bear to hear them treated with disrespect as I do,' says my lady, and took out her pocket-handkerchief; 'they are the best of friends, and if I had taken their advice—But my father was wrong to lock me up, I own. That was the only unkind thing I can charge him with; for if he had not locked me up, I should never have had a serious thought of running away as I did.'

'Well, my dear,' said my master, 'don't cry and make yourself uneasy about it now, when it's all over, and you have the man of your own choice, in spite of 'em all.'

'I was too young, I know, to make a choice at the time you ran away with me, I'm sure,' says my lady, and another sigh, which made my master, half-shaved as he was, turn round upon her in surprise.

'Why, Bell,' says he, 'you can't deny what you know as well as I do, that it was at your own particular desire, and that twice under your own hand and seal expressed, that I should carry you off as I did to Scotland, and marry you there.'

'Well, say no more about it, Sir Condy,' said my lady, pettish-like; 'I was a child then, you know.'

'And as far as I know, you're little better now, my dear Bella, to be talking in this manner to your husband's face; but I won't take it ill of you, for I know it's something in that letter you put into your pocket just now that has set you against me all on a sudden, and imposed upon your understanding.'

'It's not so very easy as you think it, Sir Condy, to impose upon my understanding,' said my lady.

'My dear,' says he, 'I have, and with reason, the best opinion of your understanding of any man now breathing; and you know I have never set my own in competition with it till now, my dear Bella,' says he, taking her hand from her book as kind as could be—'till now, when I have the great advantage of being quite cool, and you not; so don't believe one word your friends say against your own Sir Condy, and lend me the letter out of your pocket, till I see what it is they can have to say.'

'Take it then,' says she; 'and as you are quite cool, I hope it is a proper time to request you'll allow me to comply with the wishes of all my own friends, and return to live with my father and family, during the remainder of my wretched existence, at Mount Juliet's Town.'

At this my poor master fell back a few paces, like one that had been shot.

'You're not serious, Bella,' says he; 'and could you find it in your heart to leave me this way in the very middle of my distresses, all alone.' But recollecting himself after his first surprise, and a moment's time for reflection, he said, with a great deal of consideration for my lady, 'Well, Bella, my dear, I believe you are right; for what could you do at Castle Rackrent, and an execution against the goods coming down, and the furniture to be canted, and an auction in the house all next week? So you have my full consent to go, since that is your desire; only you must not think of my accompanying you, which I could not in honour do upon the terms I always have been, since our marriage, with your friends. Besides, I have business to transact at home; so in the meantime, if we are to have any breakfast this morning, let us go down and have it for the last time in peace and comfort, Bella.'

Then as I heard my master coming to the passage door, I finished fastening up my slate against the broken pane; and when he came out I wiped down the window-seat with my wig, I and bade him a 'good-morrow' as kindly as I could, seeing he was in trouble, though he strove and thought to hide it from me.

[Wigs were formerly used instead of brooms in Ireland for sweeping or dusting tables, stairs, etc. The Editor doubted the fact till he saw a labourer of the old school sweep down a flight of stairs with his wig;

he afterwards put it on his head again with the utmost composure, and said, 'Oh, please your honour, it's never a bit the worse.

It must be acknowledged that these men are not in any danger of catching cold by taking off their wigs occasionally, because they usually have fine crops of hair growing under their wigs. The wigs are often yellow, and the hair which appears from beneath them black; the wigs are usually too small, and are raised up by the hair beneath, or by the ears of the wearers.]

'This window is all racked and tattered,' says I, 'and it's what I'm striving to mend.'

'It IS all racked and tattered, plain enough,' says he, 'and never mind mending it, honest old Thady,' says he; 'it will do well enough for you and I, and that's all the company we shall have left in the house by and by.'

'I'm sorry to see your honour so low this morning,' says I; 'but you'll be better after taking your breakfast.'

'Step down to the servants' hall,' said he, 'and bring me up the pen and ink into the parlour, and get a sheet of paper from Mrs. Jane, for I have business that can't brook to be delayed; and come into the parlour with the pen and ink yourself, Thady, for I must have you to witness my signing a paper I have to execute in a hurry.'

Well, while I was getting of the pen and ink-horn, and the sheet of paper, I ransacked my brains to think what could be the papers my poor master could have to execute in such a hurry, he that never thought of such a thing as doing business afore breakfast in the whole course of his life, for any man living; but this was for my lady, as I afterwards found, and the more genteel of him after all her treatment.

I was just witnessing the paper that he had scrawled over, and was shaking the ink out of my pen upon the carpet, when my lady came in to breakfast, and she started as if it had been a ghost; as well she might, when she saw Sir Condy writing at this unseasonable hour.

'That will do very well, Thady,' says he to me, and took the paper I had signed to, without knowing what upon the earth it might be, out of my hands, and walked, folding it up, to my lady.

'You are concerned in this, my Lady Rackrent,' said he, putting it into her hands; 'and I beg you'll keep this memorandum safe, and show it to your friends the first thing you do when you get home; but put it in your pocket now, my dear, and let us eat our breakfast, in God's name.'

'What is all this?' said my lady, opening the paper in great curiosity.

'It's only a bit of a memorandum of what I think becomes me to do whenever I am able,' says my master; 'you know my situation, tied hand and foot at the present time being, but that can't last always, and when I'm dead and gone the land will be to the good, Thady, you know; and take notice it's my intention your lady should have a clear five hundred a year jointure out the estate afore any of my debts are paid.' 'Oh, please your honour,' says I, 'I can't expect to live to see that time, being now upwards of fourscore years of age, and you a young man, and likely to continue so, by the help of God.'

I was vexed to see my lady so insensible too, for all she said was, 'This is very genteel of you, Sir Condy. You need not wait any longer, Thady.' So I just picked up the pen and ink that had tumbled on the floor, and heard my master finish with saying, 'You behaved very genteel to me, my dear, when you threw all the little you had in your power along with yourself into my hands; and as I don't deny but what you may have had some things to complain of,'—to be sure he was thinking then of Judy, or of the whisky-punch, one or t'other, or both,—'and as I don't deny but you may have had something to complain of, my dear, it is but fair you should have something in the form of compensation to look forward to agreeably in future; besides, it's an act of justice to myself, that none of your friends, my dear, may ever have it to say against me, I married for money, and not for love.'

'That is the last thing I should ever have thought of saying of you, Sir Condy,' said my lady, looking very gracious.

'Then, my dear,' said Sir Condy, 'we shall part as good friends as we met; so all's right.'

I was greatly rejoiced to hear this, and went out of the parlour to report it all to the kitchen. The next morning my lady and Mrs. Jane set out for Mount Juliet's Town in the jaunting-car. Many wondered at my lady's choosing to go away, considering all things, upon the jaunting-car, as if it was only a party of pleasure; but they did not know till I told them that the coach was all broke in the journey down, and no other vehicle but the car to be had. Besides, my lady's friends were to send their coach to meet her at the cross-roads; so it was all done very proper.

My poor master was in great trouble after my lady left us. The execution came down, and everything at Castle Rackrent was seized by the gripers, and my son Jason, to his shame be it spoken, amongst them. I wondered, for the life of me, how he could harden himself to do it; but then he had been studying the law, and had made himself Attorney Quirk; so he brought down at once a heap of accounts upon my master's head. To cash lent, and to ditto, and to ditto, and to ditto and oats, and bills paid at the milliner's and linen-draper's, and many dresses for the fancy balls in Dublin for my lady, and all the bills to the workmen and tradesmen for the scenery of the theatre, and the chandler's and grocer's bills, and tailor's, besides butcher's and baker's, and, worse than all, the old one of that base wine merchant's, that wanted to arrest my poor master for the amount on the election day, for which amount Sir Condy afterwards passed his note of hand, bearing lawful interest from the date thereof; and the interest and compound interest was now mounted to a terrible deal on many other notes and bonds for money borrowed, and there was, besides, hush-money to the sub-sheriffs, and sheets upon sheets of old and new attorneys' bills, with heavy balances, 'as per former account furnished,' brought forward with interest thereon; then there was a powerful deal due to the Crown for sixteen years' arrear of quit-rent of the town-lands of Carrickshaughlin, with driver's fees, and a compliment to the receiver every year for letting the quit-rent run on to oblige Sir Condy, and Sir Kit afore him. Then there were bills for spirits and ribands at the election time, and the gentlemen of the committee's accounts unsettled, and their subscription never gathered; and there were cows to be paid for, with the smith and farrier's bills to be set against the rent of the demesne, with calf and hay money; then there was all the servants' wages, since I don't know when, coming due to them, and sums advanced for them by my son Jason for clothes, and boots, and whips, and odd moneys for sundries expended by them in journeys to town and elsewhere, and pocket-money for the master continually, and messengers and postage before his being a Parliament man. I can't myself tell you what besides; but this I know, that when the evening came on the which Sir Condy had appointed to settle all with my son Jason, and when he comes into the parlour, and sees the sight of bills and load of papers all gathered on the great dining-table for him, he puts his hands before both his eyes, and cried out, 'Merciful Jasus! what is it I see before me?' Then I sets an arm-chair at the table for him, and with a deal of difficulty he sits him down, and my son Jason hands him over the pen and ink to sign to this man's bill and t'other man's bill, all which he did without making the least objections. Indeed, to give him his due, I never seen a man more fair and honest, and easy in all his dealings, from first to last, as Sir Condy, or more willing to pay every man his own as far as he was able, which is as much as any one can do.

'Well,' says he, joking like with Jason, 'I wish we could settle it all with a stroke of my grey goose quill. What signifies making me wade through all this ocean of papers here; can't you now, who understand drawing out an account, debtor and creditor, just sit down here at the corner of the table and get it done out for me, that I may have a clear view of the balance, which is all I need be talking about, you know?'

'Very true, Sir Condy; nobody understands business better than yourself,' says Jason.

'So I've a right to do, being born and bred to the bar,' says Sir Condy. 'Thady, do step out and see are they bringing in the things for the punch, for we've just done all we have to do for this evening.'

I goes out accordingly, and when I came back Jason was pointing to the balance, which was a terrible sight to my poor master.

'Pooh! pooh! pooh!' says he. 'Here's so many noughts they dazzle my eyes, so they do, and put me in mind of all I suffered larning of my numeration table, when I was a boy at the day-school along with you, Jason—units, tens, hundreds, tens of hundreds. Is the punch ready, Thady?' says he, seeing me.

'Immediately; the boy has the jug in his hand; it's coming upstairs, please your honour, as fast as possible,' says I, for I saw his honour was tired out of his life; but Jason, very short and cruel, cuts me off with—'Don't be talking of punch yet awhile; it's no time for punch yet a bit—units, tens, hundreds,' goes he on, counting over the master's shoulder, units, tens, hundreds, thousands.

'A-a-ah! hold your hand,' cries my master. 'Where in this wide world am I to find hundreds, or units itself, let alone thousands?'

'The balance has been running on too long,' says Jason, sticking to him as I could not have done at the time, if you'd have given both the Indies and Cork to boot; 'the balance has been running on too long, and I'm distressed myself on your account, Sir Condy, for money, and the thing must be settled now on the spot, and the balance cleared off,' says Jason.

'I'll thank you if you'll only show me how,' says Sir Condy.

'There's but one way,' says Jason, 'and that's ready enough. When there's no cash, what can a gentleman do but go to the land?'

'How can you go to the land, and it under custodiam to yourself already?' says Sir Condy; 'and another custodiam hanging over it? And no one at all can touch it, you know, but the custodees.'

'Sure, can't you sell, though at a loss? Sure you can sell, and I've a purchaser ready for you,' says Jason.

'Have you so?' says Sir Condy. 'That's a great point gained. But there's a thing now beyond all, that perhaps you don't know yet, barring Thady has let you into the secret.'

'Sarrah bit of a secret, or anything at all of the kind, has he learned from me these fifteen weeks come St. John's Eve,' says I, 'for we have scarce been upon speaking terms of late. But what is it your honour means of a secret?'

'Why, the secret of the little keepsake I gave my Lady Rackrent the morning she left us, that she might not go back empty-handed to her friends.'

'My Lady Rackrent, I'm sure, has baubles and keepsakes enough, as those bills on the table will show,' says Jason; 'but whatever it is,' says he, taking up his pen, 'we must add it to the balance, for to be sure it can't be paid for.'

'No, nor can't till after my decease,' says Sir Condy; 'that's one good thing.' Then colouring up a good deal, he tells Jason of the memorandum of the five hundred a-year jointure he had settled upon my lady; at which Jason was indeed mad, and said a great deal in very high words, that it was using a gentleman who had the management of his affairs, and was, moreover, his principal creditor, extremely ill to do such a thing without consulting him, and against his knowledge and consent. To all which Sir Condy had nothing to reply, but that, upon his conscience, it was in a hurry and without a moment's thought on his part, and he was very sorry for it, but if it was to do over again he would do the same; and he appealed to me, and I was ready to give my evidence, if that would do, to the truth of all he said.

So Jason with much ado was brought to agree to a compromise.

'The purchaser that I have ready,' says he, 'will be much displeased, to be sure, at the encumbrance on the land, but I must see and manage him. Here's a deed ready drawn up; we have nothing to do but to put in the consideration money and our names to it.'

'And how much am I going to sell!—the lands of O'Shaughlin's Town, and the lands of Gruneaghoolaghan, and the lands of Crookagnawaturgh,' says he, just reading to himself. 'And—oh, murder, Jason! sure you won't put this in—the castle, stable, and appurtenances of Castle Rackrent?'

'Oh, murder!' says I, clapping my hands; 'this is too bad, Jason.'

'Why so?' said Jason. 'When it's all, and a great deal more to the back of it, lawfully mine, was I to push for it.'

'Look at him,' says I, pointing to Sir Condy, who was just leaning back in his arm-chair, with his arms falling beside him like one stupefied; 'is it you, Jason, that can stand in his presence, and recollect all he has been to us, and all we have been to him, and yet use him so at the last?'

'Who will you find to use him better, I ask you?' said Jason; 'if he can get a better purchaser, I'm content; I only offer to purchase, to make things easy, and oblige him; though I don't see what compliment I am under, if you come to that. I have never had, asked, or charged more than sixpence in the pound, receiver's fees, and where would he have got an agent for a penny less?'

'Oh, Jason! Jason! how will you stand to this in the face of the county, and all who know you?' says I; 'and what will people think and say when they see you living here in Castle Rackrent, and the lawful owner turned out of the seat of his ancestors, without a cabin to put his head into, or so much as a potato to eat?'

Jason, whilst I was saying this, and a great deal more, made me signs, and winks, and frowns; but I took no heed, for I was grieved and sick at heart for my poor master, and couldn't but speak.

'Here's the punch,' says Jason, for the door opened; 'here's the punch!'

Hearing that, my master starts up in his chair, and recollects himself, and Jason uncorks the whisky.

'Set down the jug here,' says he, making room for it beside the papers opposite to Sir Condy, but still not stirring the deed that was to make over all.

Well, I was in great hopes he had some touch of mercy about him when I saw him making the punch, and my master took a glass; but Jason put it back as he was going to fill again, saying: 'No, Sir Condy, it shan't be said of me I got your signature to this deed when you were half-seas over: you know your name and handwriting in that condition would not, if brought before the courts, benefit me a straw; wherefore, let us settle all before we go deeper into the punch-bowl.'

'Settle all as you will,' said Sir Condy, clapping his hands to his ears; 'but let me hear no more. I'm bothered to death this night.'

'You've only to sign,' said Jason, putting the pen to him.

'Take all, and be content,' said my master. So he signed; and the man who brought in the punch witnessed it, for I was not able, but crying like a child; and besides, Jason said, which I was glad of, that I was no fit witness, being so old and doting. It was so bad with me, I could not taste a drop of the punch itself, though my master himself, God bless him! in the midst of his trouble, poured out a glass for me, and brought it up to my lips.

'Not a drop; I thank your honour's honour as much as if I took it, though.' And I just set down the glass as it was, and went out, and when I got to the street door the neighbours' childer, who were playing at marbles there, seeing me in great trouble, left their play, and gathered about me to know what ailed me; and I told them all, for it was a great relief to me to speak to these poor childer, that seemed to have some natural feeling left in them; and when they were made sensible that Sir Condy was going to leave Castle Rackrent for good and all, they set up a whillaluh that could be heard to the farthest end of the street; and one—fine boy he was—that my master had given an apple to that morning, cried the loudest; but they all were the same sorry, for Sir Condy was greatly beloved amongst the childer, for letting them go a-nutting in the demesne, without saying a word to them, though my lady objected to them. The people in the town, who were the most of them standing at their doors, hearing the childer cry, would know the reason of it; and when the report was made known, the people one and all gathered in great anger against my son Jason, and terror at the notion of his coming to be landlord over them, and they cried, 'No Jason! no Jason! Sir Condy! Sir Condy! Sir Condy Rackrent for ever!' And the mob grew so great and so loud, I was frightened, and made my way back to the house to warn my son to make his escape, or hide himself for fear of the consequences. Jason would not believe me till they came all round the house, and to the windows with great shouts. Then he grew quite pale, and asked Sir Condy what had he best do?

'I'll tell you what you had best do,' said Sir Condy, who was laughing to see his fright; 'finish your glass first, then let's go to the window and show ourselves, and I'll tell 'em—or you shall, if you please—that I'm going to the Lodge for change of air for my health, and by my own desire, for the rest of my days.'

'Do so,' said Jason, who never meant it should have been so but could not refuse him the Lodge at this unseasonable time: Accordingly, Sir Condy threw up the sash and explained matters, and thanked all his friends, and bid them look in at the punchbowl, and observe that Jason and he had been sitting over it very good friends; so the mob was content, and he sent them out some whisky to drink his health, and that was the last time his honour's health was ever drunk at Castle Rackrent.

The very next day, being too proud, as he said to me, to stay an hour longer in a house that did not belong to him, he sets off to the Lodge, and I along with him not many hours after. And there was great bemoaning through all O'Shaughlin's Town, which I stayed to witness, and gave my poor master a full account of when I got to the Lodge. He was very low, and in his bed, when I got there, and complained of a great pain about his heart; but I guessed it was only trouble and all the business, let alone vexation, he had gone through of late; and knowing the nature of him from a boy, I took my pipe, and whilst smoking it by the chimney began telling him how he was beloved and regretted in the county, and it did him a deal of good to hear it.

'Your honour has a great many friends yet that you don't know of, rich and poor, in the county,' says I; 'for as I was coming along the road I met two gentlemen in their own carriages, who asked after you, knowing me, and wanted to know where you was and all about you, and even how old I was. Think of that.'

Then he wakened out of his doze, and began questioning me who the gentlemen were. And the next morning it came into my head to go, unknown to anybody, with my master's compliments, round to many of the gentlemen's houses, where he and my lady used to visit, and people that I knew were his great friends, and would go to Cork to serve him any day in the year, and I made bold to try to borrow a trifle of cash from them. They all treated me very civil for the most part, and asked a great many questions very kind about my lady and Sir Condy and all the family, and were greatly surprised to learn from me Castle Rackrent was sold, and my master at the Lodge for health; and they all pitied him greatly, and he had their good wishes, if that would do; but money was a thing they unfortunately had not any of them at this time to spare. I had my journey for my pains, and I, not used to walking, nor supple as formerly, was greatly tired, but had the satisfaction of telling my master, when I got to the Lodge, all the civil things said by high and low.

'Thady,' says he, 'all you've been telling me brings a strange thought into my head. I've a notion I shall not be long for this world anyhow, and I've a great fancy to see my own funeral afore I die.' I was greatly shocked, at the first speaking, to hear him speak so light about his funeral, and he to all appearance in good health; but recollecting myself, answered:

'To be sure it would be as fine a sight as one could see, I dared to say, and one I should be proud to witness, and I did not doubt his honour's would be as great a funeral as ever Sir Patrick O'Shaughlin's was, and such a one as that had never been known in the county afore or since.' But I never thought he was in earnest about seeing his own funeral himself till the next day he returns to it again.

'Thady,' says he, 'as far as the wake goes, sure I might without any great trouble have the satisfaction of seeing a bit of my own funeral.' [A 'wake' in England is a meeting avowedly for merriment; in Ireland it is a nocturnal meeting avowedly for the purpose of watching and bewailing the dead, but in reality for gossiping and debauchery. [GLOSSARY 28]

'Well, since your honour's honour's SO bent upon it,' says I, not willing to cross him, and he in trouble, 'we must see what we can do.'

So he fell into a sort of sham disorder, which was easy done, as he kept his bed, and no one to see him; and I got my shister, who was an old woman very handy about the sick, and very skilful, to come up to the Lodge to nurse him; and we gave out, she knowing no better, that he was just at his latter end, and it answered beyond anything; and there was a great throng of people, men, women, and childer, and there being only two rooms at the Lodge, except what was locked up full of Jason's furniture and things, the house was soon as full and fuller than it could hold, and the heat, and smoke, and noise wonderful great; and standing amongst them that were near the bed, but not thinking at all of the dead, I was startled by the sound of my master's voice from under the greatcoats that had been thrown all at top, and I went close up, no one noticing.

'Thady,' says he, 'I've had enough of this; I'm smothering, and can't hear a word of all they're saying of the deceased.'

'God bless you, and lie still and quiet,' says I, 'a bit longer, for my shister's afraid of ghosts, and would die on the spot with fright was she to see you come to life all on a sudden this way without the least preparation.'

So he lays him still, though well nigh stifled, and I made all haste to tell the secret of the joke, whispering to one and t'other, and there was a great surprise, but not so great as we had laid out it would. 'And aren't we to have the pipes and tobacco, after coming so far to-night?' said some; but they were all well enough pleased when his honour got up to drink with them, and sent for more spirits from a shebeen-house ['Shebeen-house,' a hedge alehouse. Shebeen properly means weak, small-beer, taplash.], where they very civilly let him have it upon credit. So the night passed off very merrily, but to my mind Sir Condy was rather upon the sad order in the midst of it all, not finding there had been such a great talk about himself after his death as he had always expected to hear.

The next morning, when the house was cleared of them, and none but my shister and myself left in the kitchen with Sir Condy, one opens the door and walks in, and who should it be but Judy M'Quirk herself! I forgot to notice that she had been married long since, whilst young Captain Moneygawl lived at the Lodge, to the captain's huntsman, who after a whilst 'listed and left her, and was killed in the wars. Poor Judy fell off greatly in her good looks after her being married a year or two; and being smoke-dried in the cabin, and neglecting herself like, it was hard for Sir Condy himself to know her again till she spoke; but when she says, 'It's Judy M'Quirk, please your honour; don't you remember her?'

'Oh, Judy, is it you?' says his honour. 'Yes, sure, I remember you very well; but you're greatly altered, Judy.'

'Sure it's time for me,' says she. 'And I think your honour, since I seen you last—but that's a great while ago—is altered too.'

'And with reason, Judy,' says Sir Condy, fetching a sort of a sigh. 'But how's this, Judy?' he goes on. 'I take it a little amiss of you that you were not at my wake last night.'

'Ah, don't be being jealous of that,' says she; 'I didn't hear a sentence of your honour's wake till it was all over, or it would have gone hard with me but I would have been at it, sure; but I was forced to go ten miles up the country three days ago to a wedding of a relation of my own's, and didn't get home till after the wake was over. But,' says she, 'it won't be so, I hope, the next time, please your honour.' [At the coronation of one of our monarchs the King complained of the confusion which happened in the procession. 'The great officer who presided told his Majesty that 'it should not be so next time.']

'That we shall see, Judy,' says his honour, 'and maybe sooner than you think for, for I've been very unwell this while past, and don't reckon anyway I'm long for this world.'

At this Judy takes up the corner of her apron, and puts it first to one eye and then to t'other, being to all appearance in great trouble; and my shister put in her word, and bid his honour have a good heart, for she was sure it was only the gout that Sir Patrick used to have flying about him, and he ought to drink a glass or a bottle extraordinary to keep it out of his stomach; and he promised to take her advice, and sent out for more spirits immediately; and Judy made a sign to me, and I went over to the door to her, and she said, 'I wonder to see Sir Condy so low: has he heard the news?'

'What news?' says I.

'Didn't ye hear it, then?' says she; 'my Lady Rackrent that was is kilt [See GLOSSARY 29] and lying for dead, and I don't doubt but it's all over with her by this time.'

'Mercy on us all,' says I; 'how was it?'

'The jaunting-car it was that ran away with her,' says Judy. 'I was coming home that same time from Biddy M'Guggin's marriage, and a great crowd of people too upon the road, coming from the fair of Crookaghnawaturgh, and I sees a jaunting-car standing in the middle of the road, and with the two wheels off and all tattered. "What's this?" says I. "Didn't ye hear of it?" says they that were looking on; "it's my Lady Rackrent's car, that was running away from her husband, and the horse took fright at a carrion that lay across the road, and so ran away with the jaunting-car, and my Lady Rackrent and her maid screaming, and the horse ran with them against a car that was coming from the fair with the boy asleep on it, and the lady's petticoat hanging out of the jaunting-car caught, and she was dragged I can't tell you how far upon the road, and it all broken up with the stones just going to be pounded, and one of the road-makers, with his sledge-hammer in his hand, stops the horse at the last; but my Lady Rackrent was all kilt and smashed," [KILT AND SMASHED.—Our author is not here guilty of an anti-climax. The mere English reader, from a similarity of sound between the words 'kilt' and 'killed,' might be induced to suppose that their meanings are similar, yet they are not by any means in Ireland synonymous terms. Thus you may hear a man exclaim, 'I'm kilt and murdered!' but he frequently means only that he has received a black eye or a slight contusion. 'I'm kilt all over' means that he is in a worse state than being simply 'kilt.' Thus, 'I'm kilt with the cold,' is nothing to 'I'm kilt all over with the rheumatism.'] and they lifted her into a cabin hard by, and the maid was found after where she had been thrown in the gripe of a ditch, her cap and bonnet all full of bog water, and they say my lady can't live anyway. Thady, pray now is it true what I'm told for sartain, that Sir Condy has made over all to your son Jason?'

'All,' says I.

'All entirely?' says she again.

'All entirely' says I.

'Then,' says she, 'that's a great shame; but don't be telling Jason what I say.'

'And what is it you say?' cries Sir Condy, leaning over betwixt us, which made Judy start greatly. 'I know the time when Judy M'Quirk would never have stayed so long talking at the door and I in the house.'

'Oh!' says Judy, 'for shame, Sir Condy; times are altered since then, and it's my Lady Rackrent you ought to be thinking of.'

'And why should I be thinking of her, that's not thinking of me now?' says Sir Condy.

'No matter for that,' says Judy, very properly; 'it's time you should be thinking of her, if ever you mean to do it at all, for don't you know she's lying for death?'

'My Lady Rackrent!' says Sir Condy, in a surprise; 'why it's but two days since we parted, as you very well know, Thady, in her full health and spirits, and she, and her maid along with her, going to Mount Juliet's Town on her jaunting-car.

'She'll never ride no more on her jaunting-car,' said Judy, 'for it has been the death of her, sure enough.'

And is she dead then?' says his honour.

'As good as dead, I hear,' says Judy; 'but there's Thady here as just learnt the whole truth of the story as I had it, and it's fitter he or anybody else should be telling it you than I, Sir Condy: I must be going home to the childer.'

But he stops her, but rather from civility in him, as I could see very plainly, than anything else, for Judy was, as his honour remarked at her first coming in, greatly changed, and little likely, as far as I could see—though she did not seem to be clear of it herself—little likely to be my Lady Rackrent now, should there be a second toss-up to be made. But I told him the whole story out of the face, just as Judy had told it to me, and he sent off a messenger with his compliments to Mount Juliet's Town that evening, to learn the truth of the report, and Judy bid the boy that was going call in at Tim M'Enerney's shop in O'Shaughlin's Town and buy her a new shawl.

'Do so,' Said Sir Condy, 'and tell Tim to take no money from you, for I must pay him for the shawl myself.' At this my shister throws me over a look, and I says nothing, but turned the tobacco in my mouth, whilst Judy began making a many words about it, and saying how she could not be beholden for shawls to any gentleman. I left her there to consult with my shister, did she think there was anything in it, and my shister thought I was blind to be asking her the question, and I thought my shister must see more into it than I did, and recollecting all past times and everything, I changed my mind, and came over to her way of thinking, and we settled it that Judy was very like to be my Lady Rackrent after all, if a vacancy should have happened.

The next day, before his honour was up, somebody comes with a double knock at the door, and I was greatly surprised to see it was my son Jason.

'Jason, is it you?' said I; 'what brings you to the Lodge?' says I. 'Is it my Lady Rackrent? We know that already since yesterday.'

'Maybe so,' says he; 'but I must see Sir Condy about it.'

'You can't see him yet,' says I; 'sure he is not awake.'

'What then,' says he, 'can't he be wakened, and I standing at the door?'

'I'll not: be disturbing his honour for you, Jason,' says I; 'many's the hour you've waited in your time, and been proud to do it, till his honour was at leisure to speak to you. His honour,' says I, raising my voice, at which his honour wakens of his own accord, and calls to me from the room to know who it was I was speaking to. Jason made no more ceremony, but follows me into the room.

'How are you, Sir Condy?' says he; 'I'm happy to see you looking so well; I came up to know how you did to-day, and to see did you want for anything at the Lodge?'

'Nothing at all, Mr. Jason, I thank you,' says he; for his honour had his own share of pride, and did not choose, after all that had passed, to be beholden, I suppose, to my son; 'but pray take a chair and be seated, Mr. Jason.'

Jason sat him down upon the chest, for chair there was none, and after he had set there some time, and a silence on all sides.

'What news is there stirring in the country, Mr. Jason M'Quirk?' says Sir Condy, very easy, yet high like.

'None that's news to you, Sir Condy, I hear,' says Jason. 'I am sorry to hear of my Lady Rackrent's accident.'

'I'm much obliged to you, and so is her ladyship, I'm sure,' answered Sir Condy, still stiff; and there was another sort of a silence, which seemed to lie the heaviest on my son Jason.

'Sir Condy,' says he at last, seeing Sir Condy disposing himself to go to sleep again, 'Sir Condy, I daresay you recollect mentioning to me the little memorandum you gave to Lady Rackrent about the L500 a year jointure.'

'Very true,' said Sir Condy; 'it is all in my recollection.' 'But if my Lady Rackrent dies, there's an end of all jointure,' says Jason.

'Of course,' says Sir Condy.

'But it's not a matter of certainty that my Lady Rackrent won't recover,' says Jason.

'Very true, sir,' says my master.

'It's a fair speculation, then, for you to consider what the chance of the jointure of those lands, when out of custodiam, will be to you.'

'Just five hundred a year, I take it, without any speculation at all,' said Sir Condy.

'That's supposing the life dropt, and the custodiam off, you know; begging your pardon, Sir Condy, who understands business, that is a wrong calculation.'

'Very likely so,' said Sir Condy; 'but, Mr. Jason, if you have anything to say to me this morning about it, I'd be obliged to you to say it, for I had an indifferent night's rest last night, and wouldn't be sorry to sleep a little this morning.'

'I have only three words to say, and those more of consequence to you, Sir Condy, than me. You are a little cool, I observe; but I hope you will not be offended at what I have brought here in my pocket,' and he pulls out two long rolls, and showers down golden guineas upon the bed.

'What's this?' said Sir Condy; 'it's long since'—but his pride stops him.

'All these are your lawful property this minute, Sir Condy, if you please,' said Jason.

'Not for nothing, I'm sure,' said Sir Condy, and laughs a little. 'Nothing for nothing, or I'm under a mistake with you, Jason.'

'Oh, Sir Condy, we'll not be indulging ourselves in any unpleasant retrospects,' says Jason; 'it's my present intention to behave, as I'm sure you will, like a gentleman in this affair. Here's two hundred guineas, and a third I mean to add if you should think proper to make over to me all your right and title to those lands that you know of.'

'I'll consider of it,' said my master; and a great deal more, that I was tired listening to, was said by Jason, and all that, and the sight of the ready cash upon the bed, worked with his honour; and the short and the long of it was, Sir Condy gathered up the golden guineas, and tied them up in a handkerchief, and signed some paper Jason brought with him as usual, and there was an end of the business: Jason took himself away, and my master turned himself round and fell asleep again.

I soon found what had put Jason in such a hurry to conclude this business. The little gossoon we had sent off the day before with my master's compliments to Mount Juliet's Town, and to know how my lady did after her accident, was stopped early this morning, coming back with his answer through O'Shaughlin's Town, at Castle Rackrent, by my son Jason, and questioned of all he knew of my lady from the servant at Mount Juliet's Town; and the gossoon told him my Lady Rackrent was not expected to live over night; so Jason thought it high time to be moving to the Lodge, to make his bargain with my master about the jointure afore it should be too late, and afore the little gossoon should reach us with the news. My master was greatly vexed—that is, I may say, as much as ever I seen him when he found how he had been taken in; but it was some comfort to have the ready cash for immediate consumption in the house, anyway.

And when Judy came up that evening, and brought the childer to see his honour, he unties the handkerchief, and—God bless him! whether it was little or much he had, 'twas all the same with him—he gives 'em all round guineas apiece.

'Hold up your head,' says my shister to Judy, as Sir Condy was busy filling out a glass of punch for her eldest boy—'Hold up your head, Judy; for who knows but we may live to see you yet at the head of the Castle Rackrent estate?'

'Maybe so,' says she, 'but not the way you are thinking of.'

I did not rightly understand which way Judy was looking when she made this speech till a while after.

'Why, Thady, you were telling me yesterday that Sir Condy had sold all entirely to Jason, and where then does all them guineas in the handkerchief come from?'

'They are the purchase-money of my lady's jointure,' says I.

Judy looks a little bit puzzled at this. 'A penny for your thoughts, Judy,' says my shister; 'hark, sure Sir Condy is drinking her health.'

He was at the table in the room [THE ROOM—the principal room in the house], drinking with the excise-man and the gauger, who came up to see his honour, and we were standing over the fire in the kitchen.

'I don't much care is he drinking my health or not,' says Judy; 'and it is not Sir Condy I'm thinking of, with all your jokes, whatever he is of me.'

'Sure you wouldn't refuse to be my Lady Rackrent, Judy, if you had the offer?' says I.

'But if I could do better!' says she.

'How better?' says I and my shister both at once.

'How better?' says she. 'Why, what signifies it to be my Lady Rackrent and no castle? Sure what good is the car, and no horse to draw it?'

'And where will ye get the horse, Judy?' says I.

'Never mind that,' says she; 'maybe it is your own son Jason might find that.'

'Jason!' says I; 'don't be trusting to him, Judy. Sir Condy, as I have good reason to know, spoke well of you when Jason spoke very indifferently of you, Judy.'

'No matter,' says Judy; 'it's often men speak the contrary just to what they think of us.'

'And you the same way of them, no doubt,' answered I. 'Nay, don't he denying it, Judy, for I think the better of ye for it, and shouldn't be proud to call ye the daughter of a shister's son of mine, if I was to hear ye talk ungrateful, and anyway disrespectful of his honour.'

'What disrespect,' says she, 'to say I'd rather, if it was my luck, be the wife of another man?'

'You'll have no luck, mind my words, Judy,' says I; and all I remembered about my poor master's goodness in tossing up for her afore he married at all came across me, and I had a choking in my throat that hindered me to say more.

'Better luck, anyhow, Thady,' says she, 'than to be like some folk, following the fortunes of them that have none left.'

Oh! King of Glory!' says I, 'hear the pride and ungratitude of her, and he giving his last guineas but a minute ago to her childer, and she with the fine shawl on her he made her a present of but yesterday!'

'Oh, troth, Judy, you're wrong now,' says my shister, looking at the shawl.

'And was not he wrong yesterday, then,' says she, 'to be telling me I was greatly altered, to affront me?'

'But, Judy,' says I, 'what is it brings you here then at all in the mind you are in; is it to make Jason think the better of you?'

'I'll tell you no more of my secrets, Thady,' says she, 'nor would have told you this much, had I taken you for such an unnatural fader as I find you are, not to wish your own son prefarred to another.'

'Oh, troth, you are wrong now, Thady,' says my shister.

Well, I was never so put to it in my life: between these womens, and my son and my master, and all I felt and thought just now, I could not, upon my conscience, tell which was the wrong from the right. So I said not a word more, but was only glad his honour had not the luck to hear all Judy had been saying of him, for I reckoned it would have gone nigh to break his heart; not that I was of opinion he cared for her as much as she and my shister fancied, but the ungratitude of the whole from Judy might not plase him; and he could never stand the notion of not being well spoken of or beloved like behind his back. Fortunately for all parties concerned, he was so much elevated at this time, there was no danger of his understanding anything, even if it had reached his ears. There was a great horn at the Lodge, ever since my master and Captain Moneygawl was in together, that used to belong originally to the celebrated Sir Patrick, his ancestor; and his honour was fond often of telling the story that he learned from me when a child, how Sir Patrick drank the full of this horn without stopping, and this was what no other man afore or since could without drawing breath. Now Sir Condy challenged the gauger, who seemed to think little of the horn, to swallow the contents, and had it filled to the brim with punch; and the gauger said it was what he could not do for nothing, but he'd hold Sir Condy a hundred guineas he'd do it.

'Done,' says my master; 'I'll lay you a hundred golden guineas to a tester you don't.' [TESTER: sixpence; from the French word TETE, a head—a piece of silver stamped with a head, which in old French was called UN TESTION, and which was about the value of an old English sixpence. 'Tester' is used in Shakspeare.]

'Done,' says the gauger; and done and done's enough between two gentlemen. The gauger was cast, and my master won the bet, and thought he'd won a hundred guineas, but by the wording it was adjudged to be only a tester that was his due by the exciseman. It was all one to him; he was as well pleased, and I was glad to see him in such spirits again.

The gauger—bad luck to him!—was the man that next proposed to my master to try himself, could he take at a draught the contents of the great horn.

'Sir Patrick's horn!' said his honour; 'hand it to me: I'll hold you your own bet over again I'll swallow it.'

'Done,' says the gauger; 'I'll lay ye anything at all you do no such thing.'

'A hundred guineas to sixpence I do,' says he; 'bring me the handkerchief.' I was loth, knowing he meant the handkerchief with the gold in it, to bring it out in such company, and his honour not very able to reckon it. 'Bring me the handkerchief, then, Thady,' says he, and stamps with his foot; so with that I pulls it out of my greatcoat pocket, where I had put it for safety. Oh, how it grieved me to see the guineas counting upon the table, and they the last my master had! Says Sir Condy to me, 'Your hand is steadier than mine to-night, old Thady, and that's a wonder; fill you the horn for me.' And so, wishing his honour success, I did; but I filled it, little thinking of what would befall him. He swallows it down, and drops like one shot. We lifts him up, and he was speechless, and quite black in the face. We put him to bed, and in a short time he wakened, raving with a fever on his brain. He was shocking either to see or hear.

'Judy! Judy! have you no touch of feeling? Won't you stay to help us nurse him?' says I to her, and she putting on her shawl to go out of the house.

'I'm frightened to see him,' says she, 'and wouldn't nor couldn't stay in it; and what use? He can't last till the morning.' With that she ran off. There was none but my shister and myself left near him of all the many friends he had.

The fever came and went, and came and went, and lasted five days, and the sixth he was sensible for a few minutes, and said to me, knowing me very well, 'I'm in a burning pain all withinside of me, Thady.' I could not speak, but my shister asked him would he have this thing or t'other to do him good? 'No,' says he, 'nothing will do me good no more,' and he gave a terrible screech with the torture he was in; then again a minute's ease—'brought to this by drink,' says he. 'Where are all the friends?—where's Judy? Gone, hey? Ay, Sir Condy has been a fool all his days,' said he; and there was the last word he spoke, and died. He had but a very poor funeral after all.

If you want to know any more, I'm not very well able to tell you; but my Lady Rackrent did not die, as was expected of her, but was only disfigured in the face ever after by the fall and bruises she got; and she and Jason, immediately after my poor master's death, set about going to law about that jointure; the memorandum not being on stamped paper, some say it is worth nothing, others again it may do; others say Jason won't have the lands at any rate; many wishes it so. For my part, I'm tired wishing for anything in this world, after all I've seen in it; but I'll say nothing—it would be a folly to be getting myself ill-will in my old age. Jason did not marry, nor think of marrying Judy, as I prophesied, and I am not sorry for it: who is? As for all I have here set down from memory and hearsay of the family, there's nothing but truth in it from beginning to end. That you may depend upon, for where's the use of telling lies about the things which everybody knows as well as I do?

The Editor could have readily made the catastrophe of Sir Condy's history more dramatic and more pathetic, if he thought it allowable to varnish the plain round tale of faithful Thady. He lays it before the English reader as a specimen of manners and characters which are perhaps unknown in England. Indeed, the domestic habits of no nation in Europe were less known to the English than those of their sister country, till within these few years.

Mr. Young's picture of Ireland, in his tour through that country, was the first faithful portrait of its inhabitants. All the features in the foregoing sketch were taken from the life, and they are characteristic of that mixture of quickness, simplicity, cunning, carelessness, dissipation, disinterestedness, shrewdness, and blunder, which, in different forms and with various success, has been brought upon the stage or delineated in novels.

It is a problem of difficult solution to determine whether a union will hasten or retard the amelioration of this country. The few gentlemen of education who now reside in this country will resort to England. They are few, but they are in nothing inferior to men of the same rank in Great Britain. The best that can happen will be the introduction of British manufacturers in their places.

Did the Warwickshire militia, who were chiefly artisans, teach the Irish to drink beer? or did they learn from the Irish to drink whisky?

## GLOSSARY

*SOME FRIENDS, WHO HAVE SEEN THADY'S HISTORY SINCE IT HAS BEEN PRINTED HAVE SUGGESTED TO THE EDITOR, THAT MANY OF THE TERMS AND IDIOMATIC PHRASES, WITH WHICH IT ABOUNDS, COULD NOT BE INTELLIGIBLE TO THE ENGLISH READER WITHOUT FURTHER EXPLANATION. THE EDITOR HAS THEREFORE FURNISHED THE FOLLOWING GLOSSARY.*

### GLOSSARY 1. MONDAY MORNING—

*Thady begins his memoirs of the Rackrent Family by dating MONDAY MORNING, because no great undertaking can be auspiciously commenced in Ireland on any morning but MONDAY MORNING. 'Oh, please God we live till Monday morning, we'll set the slater to mend the roof of the house. On Monday morning we'll fall to, and cut the turf. On Monday morning we'll see and begin mowing. On Monday morning, please your honour, we'll begin and dig the potatoes,' etc.*

*All the intermediate days, between the making of such speeches and the ensuing Monday, are wasted: and when Monday morning comes, it is ten to one that the business is deferred to THE NEXT Monday morning. The Editor knew a gentleman, who, to counteract this prejudice, made his workmen and labourers begin all new pieces of work upon a Saturday.*

### GLOSSARY 2. LET ALONE THE THREE KINGDOMS ITSELF.

*—Let alone, in this sentence, means put out of consideration. The phrase, let alone, which is now used as the imperative of a verb, may in time become a conjunction, and may exercise the ingenuity of some future etymologist. The celebrated Horne Tooke has proved most satisfactorily, that the conjunction but comes from the imperative of the Anglo-Saxon verb (BEOUTAN) TO BE OUT; also, that IF comes from GIF, the imperative of the Anglo-Saxon verb which signifies TO GIVE, etc.*

**GLOSSARY 3. WHILLALUH.**

*—Ullaloo, Gol, or lamentation over the dead—*

*Magnoque ululante tumultu.—VIRGIL.*

*Ululatibus omne*
*Implevere nemus.—OVID.*

*A full account of the Irish Gol, or Ullaloo, and of the Caoinan or Irish funeral song, with its first semichorus, second semichorus, full chorus of sighs and groans, together with the Irish words and music, may be found in the fourth volume of the TRANSACTIONS OF THE ROYAL IRISH ACADEMY. For the advantage of LAZY readers, who would rather read a page than walk a yard, and from compassion, not to say sympathy, with their infirmity, the Editor transcribes the following passages:—*

*'The Irish have been always remarkable for their funeral lamentations; and this peculiarity has been noticed by almost every traveller who visited them; and it seems derived from their Celtic ancestors, the primaeval inhabitants of this isle. . . .*

*'It has been affirmed of the Irish, that to cry was more natural to them than to any other nation, and at length the Irish cry became proverbial. . . . .*

*'Cambrensis in the twelfth century says, the Irish then musically expressed their griefs; that is, they applied the musical art, in which they excelled all others, to the orderly celebration of funeral obsequies, by dividing the mourners into two bodies, each alternately singing their part, and the whole at times joining in full chorus. . . . The body of the deceased, dressed in grave clothes, and ornamented with flowers, was placed on a bier, or some elevated spot. The relations and keepers (SINGING MOURNERS) ranged themselves in two divisions, one at the head, and the other at the feet of the corpse. The bards and croteries had before prepared the funeral Caoinan. The chief bard of the head chorus began by singing the first stanza, in a low, doleful tone, which was softly accompanied by the harp: at the conclusion, the foot semichorus began the lamentation, or Ullaloo, from the final note of the preceding stanza, in which they were answered by the head semichorus; then both united in one general chorus. The chorus of the first stanza being ended, the chief bard of the foot semichorus began the second Gol or lamentation, in which he was answered by that of the head; and then, as before, both united in the general full chorus. Thus alternately were the song and choruses performed during the night. The genealogy, rank, possessions, the virtues and vices of the dead were rehearsed, and a number of interrogations were addressed to the deceased; as, Why did he die? If married, whether his wife was faithful to him, his sons dutiful, or good hunters or warriors? If a woman, whether her daughters were fair or chaste? If a young man, whether he had been crossed in love; or if the blue-eyed maids of Erin treated him with scorn?'*

*We are told, that formerly the feet (the metrical feet) of the Caoinan were much attended to; but on the decline of the Irish bards these feet were gradually neglected, and the Caoinan fell into a sort of slipshod metre amongst women. Each province had different Caoinans, or at least different imitations of the original. There was the Munster cry, the Ulster cry, etc. It became an extempore performance, and every set of keepers varied the melody according to their own fancy.*

It is curious to observe how customs and ceremonies degenerate. The present Irish cry, or howl, cannot boast of such melody, nor is the funeral procession conducted with much dignity. The crowd of people who assemble at these funerals sometimes amounts to a thousand, often to four or five hundred. They gather as the bearers of the hearse proceed on their way, and when they pass through any village, or when they come near any houses, they begin to cry—Oh! Oh! Oh! Oh! Oh! Agh! Agh! raising their notes from the first OH! to the last AGH! in a kind of mournful howl. This gives notice to the inhabitants of the village that a FUNERAL IS PASSING and immediately they flock out to follow it. In the province of Munster it is a common thing for the women to follow a funeral, to join in the universal cry with all their might and main for some time, and then to turn and ask—'Arrah! who is it that's dead?—who is it we're crying for?' Even the poorest people have their own burying-places—that is, spots of ground in the churchyards where they say that their ancestors have been buried ever since the wars of Ireland; and if these burial-places are ten miles from the place where a man dies, his friends and neighbours take care to carry his corpse thither. Always one priest, often five or six priests, attend these funerals; each priest repeats a mass, for which he is paid, sometimes a shilling, sometimes half a crown, sometimes half a guinea, or a guinea, according to their circumstances, or, as they say, according to the ability of the deceased. After the burial of any very poor man, who has left a widow or children, the priest makes what is called a COLLECTION for the widow; he goes round to every person present, and each contributes sixpence or a shilling, or what they please. The reader will find in the note upon the word WAKE, more particulars respecting the conclusion of the Irish funerals.

Certain old women, who cry particularly loud and well are in great request, and, as a man said to the Editor, 'Every one would wish and be proud to have such at his funeral, or at that of his friends.' The lower Irish are wonderfully eager to attend the funerals of their friends and relations, and they make their relationships branch out to a great extent. The proof that a poor man has been well beloved during his life is his having a crowded funeral. To attend a neighbour's funeral is a cheap proof of humanity, but it does not, as some imagine, cost nothing. The time spent in attending funerals may be safely valued at half a million to the Irish nation; the Editor thinks that double that sum would not be too high an estimate. The habits of profligacy and drunkenness which are acquired at WAKES are here put out of the question. When a labourer, a carpenter, or a smith, is not at his work, which frequently happens, ask where he is gone, and ten to one the answer is—'Oh, faith, please your honour, he couldn't do a stroke to-day, for he's gone to THE funeral.'

Even beggars, when they grow old, go about begging FOR THEIR OWN FUNERALS that is, begging for money to buy a coffin, candles, pipes, and tobacco. For the use of the candles, pipes, and tobacco, see WAKE.

Those who value customs in proportion to their antiquity, and nations in proportion to their adherence to ancient customs, will doubtless admire the Irish ULLALOO, and the Irish nation, for persevering in this usage from time immemorial. The Editor, however, has observed some alarming symptoms, which seem to prognosticate the declining taste for the Ullaloo in Ireland. In a comic theatrical entertainment, represented not long since on the Dublin stage, a chorus of old women was introduced, who set up the Irish howl round the relics of a physician, who is supposed to have fallen under the wooden sword of Harlequin. After the old women have continued their Ullaloo for a decent time, with all the necessary accompaniments of wringing their hands, wiping or rubbing their eyes with the corners of their gowns or aprons, etc., one of the mourners suddenly suspends her lamentable cries, and, turning to her neighbour, asks, 'Arrah now, honey, who is it we're crying for?'

## GLOSSARY 4. THE TENANTS WERE SENT AWAY WITHOUT THEIR WHISKY.

—It is usual with some landlords to give their inferior tenants a glass of whisky when they pay their rents. Thady calls it THEIR whisky; not that the whisky is actually the property of the tenants, but that it becomes their RIGHT after it has been often given to them. In this general mode of reasoning respecting RIGHTS the lower Irish are not singular, but they are peculiarly quick and tenacious in claiming these rights. 'Last year your honour gave me some straw for the roof of my house and I EXPECT your honour will be after doing the same this year.' In this manner gifts are frequently turned into tributes. The high and low are not always dissimilar in their habits. It is said, that the Sublime Ottoman Port is very apt to claim gifts as tributes: thus it is dangerous to send the Grand Seignor a fine horse on his birthday one year, lest on his next birthday he should expect a similar present, and should proceed to demonstrate the reasonableness of his expectations.

## GLOSSARY 5. HE DEMEANED HIMSELF GREATLY—

Means, he lowered or disgraced himself much.

## GLOSSARY 6. DUTY FOWLS, DUTY TURKEYS, AND DUTY GEESE.—

In many leases in Ireland, tenants were formerly bound to supply an inordinate quantity of poultry to their landlords. The Editor knew of thirty turkeys being reserved in one lease of a small farm.

## GLOSSARY 7. ENGLISH TENANTS.—

An English tenant does not mean a tenant who is an Englishman, but a tenant who pays his rent the day that it is due. It is a common prejudice in Ireland, amongst the poorer classes of people, to believe that all tenants in England pay their rents on the very day when they become due. An Irishman, when he goes to take a farm, if he wants to prove to his landlord that he is a substantial man, offers to become an ENGLISH TENANT. If a tenant disobliges his landlord by voting against him, or against his opinion, at an election, the tenant is immediately informed by the agent that he must become an ENGLISH TENANT. This threat does not imply that he is to change his language or his country, but that he must pay all the arrear of rent which he owes, and that he must thenceforward pay his rent on that day when it becomes due.

## GLOSSARY 8. CANTING—

Does not mean talking or writing hypocritical nonsense, but selling substantially by auction.

## GLOSSARY 9. DUTY WORK.—

It was formerly common in Ireland to insert clauses in leases, binding tenants to furnish their landlords with labourers and horses for several days in the year. Much petty tyranny and oppression have resulted from this feudal custom. Whenever a poor man disobliged his landlord, the agent sent to him for his duty work; and Thady does not exaggerate when he says, that the tenants were often called from their own work to do that of their landlord. Thus the very means of earning their rent were taken from them: whilst they were getting home their landlord's harvest, their own was often ruined, and yet their rents were expected to be paid as punctually as if their time had been at their own disposal. This appears the height of absurd injustice.

In Esthonia, amongst the poor Sclavonian race of peasant slaves, they pay tributes to their lords, not under the name of duty work, duty geese, duty turkeys, etc., but under the name of RIGHTEOUSNESSES. The following ballad is a curious specimen of Esthonian poetry:—

This is the cause that the country is ruined,
And the straw of the thatch is eaten away,
The gentry are come to live in the land—
Chimneys between the village,
And the proprietor upon the white floor!
The sheep brings forth a lamb with a white forehead,
This is paid to the lord for a RIGHTEOUSNESS SHEEP.
The sow farrows pigs,
They go to the spit of the lord.
The hen lays eggs,
They go into the lord's frying-pan.
The cow drops a male calf,
That goes into the lord's herd as a bull.
The mare foals a horse foal,
That must be for my lord's nag.
The boor's wife has sons,
They must go to look after my lord's poultry.


## GLOSSARY 10. OUT OF FORTY-NINE SUITS WHICH HE HAD, HE NEVER LOST ONE BUT SEVENTEEN.

—Thady's language in this instance is a specimen of a mode of rhetoric common in Ireland. An astonishing assertion is made in the beginning of a sentence, which ceases to be in the least surprising, when you hear the qualifying explanation that follows. Thus a man who is in the last stage of staggering drunkenness will, if he can articulate, swear to you—'Upon his conscience now, and may he never stir from the spot alive if he is telling a lie, upon his conscience he has not tasted a drop of anything, good or bad, since morning at-all-at-all, but half a pint of whisky, please your honour.'


## GLOSSARY 11. FAIRY MOUNTS

—Barrows. It is said that these high mounts were of great service to the natives of Ireland when Ireland was invaded by the Danes. Watch was always kept on them, and upon the approach of an enemy a fire was lighted to give notice to the next watch, and thus the intelligence was quickly communicated through the country. SOME YEARS AGO, the common people believed that these barrows were inhabited by fairies, or, as they called them, by the GOOD PEOPLE. 'Oh, troth, to the best of my belief, and to the best of my judgment and opinion,' said an elderly man to the Editor, 'it was only the old people that had nothing to do, and got together, and were telling stories about them fairies, but to the best of my judgment there's nothing in it. Only this I heard myself not very many years back from a decent kind of a man, a grazier, that, as he was coming just FAIR AND EASY (QUIETLY) from the fair, with some cattle and sheep, that he had not sold, just at the church of —-at an angle of the road like, he was met by a good-looking man, who asked him where he was going? And he answered, "Oh, far enough, I must be going all night." "No, that you mustn't nor won't (says the man), you'll sleep with me the night, and you'll want for nothing, nor your cattle nor sheep neither, nor your BEAST (HORSE); so come along with me." With that the grazier LIT (ALIGHTED) from his horse, and it was dark night; but presently he finds himself, he does not know in the wide world how, in a fine house, and plenty of everything to eat and drink; nothing at all wanting that he could wish for or think of. And he does not MIND (RECOLLECT or KNOW) how at last he falls asleep; and in the morning he finds himself lying, not in ever a bed or a house at all, but just in the angle of the road where first he met the strange man: there he finds himself lying on his back on the grass, and all his sheep feeding as quiet as ever all round about him, and his horse the same way, and the bridle of the beast over his wrist. And I asked him what he thought of it; and from first to last he could think of nothing, but for certain sure it must have been the fairies that entertained him so well. For there was no house to see anywhere nigh hand, or any building, or barn, or place at all, but only the church and the MOTE (BARROW). There's another odd thing enough that they tell about this same church, that if any person's corpse, that had not a right to be buried in that churchyard, went to be burying there in it, no, not all the men, women, or childer in all Ireland could get the corpse anyway into the churchyard; but as they would be trying to go into the churchyard, their feet would seem to be going backwards instead of forwards; ay, continually backwards the whole funeral would seem to go; and they would never set foot with the corpse in the churchyard. Now they say that it is the fairies do all this; but it is my opinion it is all idle talk, and people are after being wiser now.

The country people in Ireland certainly HAD great admiration mixed with reverence, if not dread, of fairies. They believed that beneath these fairy mounts were spacious subterraneous palaces, inhabited by THE GOOD PEOPLE, who must not on any account be disturbed. When the wind raises a little eddy of dust upon the road, the poor people believe that it is raised by the fairies, that it is a sign that they are journeying from one of the fairies' mounts to another, and they say to the fairies, or to the dust as it passes, 'God speed ye, gentlemen; God speed ye.' This averts any evil that THE GOOD PEOPLE might be inclined to do them. There are innumerable stories told of the friendly and unfriendly feats of these busy fairies; some of these tales are ludicrous, and some romantic enough for poetry. It is a pity that poets should lose such convenient, though diminutive machinery. By the bye, Parnell, who showed himself so deeply 'skilled in faerie lore,' was an Irishman; and though he has presented his fairies to the world in the ancient English dress of 'Britain's isle, and Arthur's days,' it is probable that his first acquaintance with them began in his native country.

Some remote origin for the most superstitious or romantic popular illusions or vulgar errors may often be discovered. In Ireland, the old churches and churchyards have been usually fixed upon as the scenes of wonders. Now antiquaries tell us, that near the ancient churches in that kingdom caves of various constructions have from time to time been discovered, which were formerly used as granaries or magazines by the ancient inhabitants, and as places to which they retreated in time of danger. There is (p.84 of the R. I. A. TRANSACTIONS for 1789) a particular account of a number of these artificial caves at the west end of the church of Killossy, in the county of Kildare. Under a rising ground, in a dry sandy soil, these subterraneous dwellings were found: they have pediment roofs, and they communicate with each other by small apertures. In the Brehon laws these are mentioned, and there are fines inflicted by those laws upon persons who steal from the subterraneous granaries. All these things show that there was a real foundation for the stories which were told of the appearance of lights, and of the sounds of voices, near these places. The persons who had property concealed there, very willingly countenanced every wonderful relation that tended to make these places objects of sacred awe or superstitious terror.

## GLOSSARY 12. WEED ASHES.

—By ancient usage in Ireland, all the weeds on a farm belonged to the farmer's wife, or to the wife of the squire who holds the ground in his own hands. The great demand for alkaline salts in bleaching rendered these ashes no inconsiderable perquisite.

## GLOSSARY 13. SEALING MONEY.

—Formerly it was the custom in Ireland for tenants to give the squire's lady from two to fifty guineas as a perquisite upon the sealing of their leases. The Editor not very long since knew of a baronet's lady accepting fifty guineas as sealing money, upon closing a bargain for a considerable farm.

## GLOSSARY 14. SIR MURTAGH GREW MAD

—Sir Murtagh grew angry.

## GLOSSARY 15. THE WHOLE KITCHEN WAS OUT ON THE STAIRS

—means that all the inhabitants of the kitchen came out of the kitchen, and stood upon the stairs. These, and similar expressions, show how much the Irish are disposed to metaphor and amplification.

## GLOSSARY 16. FINING DOWN THE YEAR'S RENT.

—When an Irish gentleman, like Sir Kit Rackrent, has lived beyond his income, and finds himself distressed for ready money, tenants obligingly offer to take his land at a rent far below the value, and to pay him a small sum of money in hand, which they call fining down the yearly rent. The temptation of this ready cash often blinds the landlord to his future interest.

## GLOSSARY 17. DRIVER.

—A man who is employed to drive tenants for rent; that is, to drive the cattle belonging to tenants to pound. The office of driver is by no means a sinecure.

## GLOSSARY 18. I THOUGHT TO MAKE HIM A PRIEST.

—It was customary amongst those of Thady's rank in Ireland, whenever they could get a little money, to send their sons abroad to St. Omer's, or to Spain, to be educated as priests. Now they are educated at Maynooth. The Editor has lately known a young lad, who began by being a post-boy, afterwards turn into a carpenter, then quit his plane and work-bench to study his HUMANITIES, as he said, at the college of Maynooth; but after he had gone through his course of Humanities, he determined to be a soldier instead of a priest.

### GLOSSARY 19. FLAM.

—Short for flambeau.

### GLOSSARY 20. BARRACK-ROOM.

—Formerly it was customary, in gentlemen's houses in Ireland, to fit up one large bedchamber with a number of beds for the reception of occasional visitors. These rooms were called Barrack-rooms.

### GLOSSARY 21. AN INNOCENT

—in Ireland, means a simpleton, an idiot.

### GLOSSARY 22. THE CURRAGH

—is the Newmarket of Ireland.

### GLOSSARY 23. THE CANT

—The auction.

### GLOSSARY 24. AND SO SHOULD CUT HIM OFF FOR EVER BY LEVYING A FINE, AND SUFFERING A RECOVERY TO DOCK THE ENTAIL.

—The English reader may perhaps be surprised at the extent of Thady's legal knowledge, and at the fluency with which he pours forth law-terms; but almost every poor man in Ireland, be he farmer, weaver, shopkeeper, ox steward, is, besides his other occupations, occasionally a lawyer. The nature of processes, ejectments, custodiams, injunctions, replevins, etc., is perfectly known to them, and the terms as familiar to them as to any attorney. They all love law. It is a kind of lottery, in which every man, staking his own wit or cunning against his neighbour's property, feels that he has little to lose, and much to gain.

'I'll have the law of you, so I will!' is the saying of an Englishman who expects justice. 'I'll have you before his honour,' is the threat of an Irishman who hopes for partiality. Miserable is the life of a justice of the peace in Ireland the day after a fair, especially if he resides near a small town. The multitude of the KILT (KILT does not mean KILLED, but hurt) and wounded who come before his honour with black eyes or bloody heads is astonishing: but more astonishing is the number of those who, though they are scarcely able by daily labour to procure daily food, will nevertheless, without the least reluctance, waste six or seven hours of the day lounging in the yard or court of a justice of the peace, waiting to make some complaint about—nothing. It is impossible to convince them that TIME IS MONEY. They do not set any value upon their own time, and they think that others estimate theirs at less than nothing. Hence they make no scruple of telling a justice of the peace a story of an hour long about a tester (sixpence); and if he grows impatient, they attribute it to some secret prejudice which he entertains against them.

Their method is to get a story completely by heart, and to tell it, as they call it, OUT OF THE FACE, that is, from the beginning to the end, without interruption.

'Well, my good friend, I have seen you lounging about these three hours in the yard; what is your business?'

'Please your honour, it is what I want to speak one word to your honour.'

'Speak then, but be quick. What is the matter?'

'The matter, please your honour, is nothing at-all-at-all, only just about the grazing of a horse, please your honour, that this man here sold me at the fair of Gurtishannon last Shrove fair, which lay down three times with myself, please your honour, and KILT me; not to be telling your honour of how, no later back than yesterday night, he lay down in the house there within, and all the childer standing round, and it was God's mercy he did not fall a-top of them, or into the fire to burn himself. So please your honour, to-day I took him back to this man, which owned him, and after a great deal to do, I got the mare again I SWOPPED (EXCHANGED) him for; but he won't pay the grazing of the horse for the time I had him, though he promised to pay the grazing in case the horse didn't answer; and he never did a day's work, good or bad, please your honour, all the time he was with me, and I had the doctor to him five times anyhow. And so, please your honour, it is what I expect your honour will stand my friend, for I'd sooner come to your honour for justice than to any other in all Ireland. And so I brought him here before your honour, and expect your honour will make him pay me the grazing, or tell me, can I process him for it at the next assizes, please your honour?'

The defendant now turning a quid of tobacco with his tongue into some secret cavern in his mouth, begins his defence with—

'Please your honour, under favour, and saving your honour's presence, there's not a word of truth in all this man has been saying from beginning to end, upon my conscience, and I wouldn't for the value of the horse itself, grazing and all, be after telling your honour a lie. For, please your honour, I have a dependence upon your honour that you'll do me justice, and not be listening to him or the like of him. Please your honour, it's what he has brought me before your honour, because he had a spite against me about some oats I sold your honour, which he was jealous of, and a shawl his wife got at my shister's shop there without, and never paid for; so I offered to set the shawl against the grazing, and give him a receipt in full of all demands, but he wouldn't out of spite, please your honour; so he brought me before your honour, expecting your honour was mad with me for cutting down the tree in the horse park, which was none of my doing, please your honour—ill-luck to them that went and belied me to your honour behind my back! So if your honour is pleasing, I'll tell you the whole truth about the horse that he swopped against my mare out of the face. Last Shrove fair I met this man, Jemmy Duffy, please your honour, just at the corner of the road, where the bridge is broken down, that your honour is to have the presentment for this year—long life to you for it! And he was at that time coming from the fair of Gurtishannon, and I the same way. "How are you, Jemmy?" says I. "Very well, I thank ye kindly, Bryan," says he; "shall we turn back to Paddy Salmon's and take a naggin of whisky to our better acquaintance?" "I don't care if I did, Jemmy," says I; "only it is what I can't take the whisky, because I'm under an oath against it for a month." Ever since, please your honour, the day your honour met me on the road, and observed to me I could hardly stand, I had taken so much; though upon my conscience your honour wronged me greatly that same time—ill-luck to them that belied me behind my back to your honour! Well, please your honour, as I was telling you, as he was taking the whisky, and we talking of one thing or t'other, he makes me an offer to swop his mare that he couldn't sell at the fair of Gurtishannon, because nobody would be troubled with the beast, please your honour, against my horse, and to oblige him I took the mare—sorrow take her! and him along with her! She kicked me a new car, that was worth three pounds ten, to tatters the first time I ever put her into it, and I expect your honour will make him pay me the price of the car, anyhow, before I pay the grazing, which I've no right to pay at-all-at-all, only to oblige him. But I leave it all to your honour; and the whole grazing he ought to be charging for the beast is but two and eightpence halfpenny, anyhow, please your honour. So I'll abide by what your honour says, good or bad. I'll leave it all to your honour."

I'll leave IT all to your honour—literally means, I'll leave all the trouble to your honour.

The Editor knew a justice of the peace in Ireland who had such a dread of HAVING IT ALL LEFT TO HIS HONOUR, that he frequently gave the complainants the sum about which they were disputing, to make peace between them, and to get rid of the trouble of hearing their stories OUT OF THE FACE. But he was soon cured of this method of buying off disputes, by the increasing multitude of those who, out of pure regard to his honour, came 'to get justice from him, because they would sooner come before him than before any man in all Ireland.'


### GLOSSARY 25. A RAKING POT OF TEA.

—We should observe, this custom has long since been banished from the higher orders of Irish gentry. The mysteries of a raking pot of tea, like those of the Bona Dea, are supposed to be sacred to females; but now and then it has happened that some of the male species, who were either more audacious, or more highly favoured than the rest of their sex, have been admitted by stealth to these orgies. The time when the festive ceremony begins varies according to circumstances, but it is never earlier than twelve o'clock at night; the joys of a raking pot of tea depending on its being made in secret, and at an unseasonable hour. After a ball, when the more discreet part of the company has departed to rest, a few chosen female spirits, who have footed it till they can foot it no longer, and till the sleepy notes expire under the slurring hand of the musician, retire to a bedchamber, call the favourite maid, who alone is admitted, bid her PUT DOWN THE KETTLE, lock the door, and amidst as much giggling and scrambling as possible, they get round a tea-table, on which all manner of things are huddled together. Then begin mutual railleries and mutual confidences amongst the young ladies, and the faint scream and the loud laugh is heard, and the romping for letters and pocket-books begins, and gentlemen are called by their surnames, or by the general name of fellows! pleasant fellows! charming fellows! odious fellows! abominable fellows! and then all prudish decorums are forgotten, and then we might be convinced how much the satirical poet was mistaken when he said—

There is no woman where there's no reserve.

The merit of the original idea of a raking pot of tea evidently belongs to the washerwoman and the laundry-maid. But why should not we have LOW LIFE ABOVE STAIRS as well as HIGH LIFE BELOW STAIRS?

**GLOSSARY 26. WE GAINED THE DAY BY THIS PIECE OF HONESTY.**

—In a dispute which occurred some years ago in Ireland, between Mr. E. and Mr. M., about the boundaries of a farm, an old tenant of Mr. M.'s cut a SOD from Mr. M.'s land, and inserted it in a spot prepared for its reception in Mr. E.'s land; so nicely was it inserted, that no eye could detect the junction of the grass. The old man, who was to give his evidence as to the property, stood upon the inserted sod when the VIEWERS came, and swore that the ground he THEN STOOD UPON belonged to his landlord, Mr. M.

The Editor had flattered himself that the ingenious contrivance which Thady records, and the similar subterfuge of this old Irishman, in the dispute concerning boundaries, were instances of 'CUTENESS unparalleled in all but Irish story: an English friend, however, has just mortified the Editor's national vanity by an account of the following custom, which prevails in part of Shropshire. It is discreditable for women to appear abroad after the birth of their children till they have been CHURCHED. To avoid this reproach, and at the same time to enjoy the pleasure of gadding, whenever a woman goes abroad before she has been to church, she takes a tile from the roof of her house, and puts it upon her head: wearing this panoply all the time she pays her visits, her conscience is perfectly at ease; for she can afterwards safely declare to the clergyman, that she 'has never been from under her own roof till she came to be churched.'

**GLOSSARY 27. CARTON AND HALF-CARTON,**

—Thady means cartron, and half-cartron. According to the old record in the black book of Dublin, a CANTRED is said to contain 30 VILLATAS TERRAS, which are also called QUARTERS of land (quarterons, CARTRONS); every one of which quarters must contain so much ground as will pasture 400 cows, and 17 plough-lands. A knight's fee was composed of 8 hydes, which amount to 160 acres, and that is generally deemed about a PLOUGH- LAND.'

The Editor was favoured by a learned friend with the above extract, from a MS. of Lord Totness's in the Lambeth library.

**GLOSSARY 28. WAKE.**

—A wake in England means a festival held upon the anniversary of the saint of the parish. At these wakes, rustic games, rustic conviviality, and rustic courtship, are pursued with all the ardour and all the appetite which accompany such pleasures as occur but seldom. In Ireland a wake is a midnight meeting, held professedly for the indulgence of holy sorrow, but usually it is converted into orgies of unholy joy. When an Irish man or woman of the lower order dies, the straw which composed the bed, whether it has been contained in a bag to form a mattress, or simply spread upon the earthen floor, is immediately taken out of the house, and burned before the cabin door, the family at the same time setting up the death howl. The ears and eyes of the neighbours being thus alarmed, they flock to the house of the deceased, and by their vociferous sympathy excite and at the same time soothe the sorrows of the family.

*It is curious to observe how good and bad are mingled in human institutions. In countries which were thinly inhabited, this custom prevented private attempts against the lives of individuals, and formed a kind of coroner's inquest upon the body which had recently expired, and burning the straw upon which the sick man lay became a simple preservative against infection. At night the dead body is waked, that is to say, all the friends and neighbours of the deceased collect in a barn or stable, where the corpse is laid upon some boards, or an unhinged door, supported upon stools, the face exposed, the rest of the body covered with a white sheet. Round the body are stuck in brass candlesticks, which have been borrowed perhaps at five miles' distance, as many candles as the poor person can beg or borrow, observing always to have an odd number. Pipes and tobacco are first distributed, and then, according to the ABILITY of the deceased, cakes and ale, and sometimes whisky, are DEALT to the company—*

*Deal on, deal on, my merry men all,*
*Deal on your cakes and your wine,*
*For whatever is dealt at her funeral to-day*
*Shall be dealt to-morrow at mine.*

*After a fit of universal sorrow, and the comfort of a universal dram, the scandal of the neighbourhood, as in higher circles, occupies the company. The young lads and lasses romp with one another, and when the fathers and mothers are at last overcome with sleep and whisky (VINO ET SOMNO), the youth become more enterprising, and are frequently successful. It is said that more matches are made at wakes than at weddings.*

### GLOSSARY 29. KILT.

*—This word frequently occurs in the preceding pages, where it means not KILLED, but much HURT. In Ireland, not only cowards, but the brave 'die many times before their death.'—There KILLING IS NO MURDER.*

## Maria Edgeworth – A Short Biography

Maria Edgeworth was born at Black Bourton, Oxfordshire on January 1st 1768, the second child of Richard Lovell Edgeworth and Anna Maria Edgeworth (née Elers).

Her early years were with her mother's family in England. Sadly, her mother died when Maria was only five. When her father married his second wife, Honora Sneyd, in 1773, the family went to live at his estate, Edgeworthstown, in County Longford, Ireland.

Maria was later sent to Mrs. Lattafière's school in Derby after Honora fell ill in 1775. There she studied dancing, French and other subjects. After Honora died in 1780 Maria's father married Honora's sister, Elizabeth, causing much social disapproved.

Maria transferred to Mrs. Devis's school in Upper Wimpole Street, London. Her father began to focus more attention on Maria in 1781 when she nearly lost her sight to an eye infection.

She returned home to Ireland at 14, and took charge of her younger siblings. She herself was home-tutored by her father in Irish economics and politics, science, literature and law. Despite her youth literature was in her blood.

She became her father's assistant in managing the Edgeworthstown estate, which had become run-down during the family's absence. Maria would now live and write there for the rest of her life.

With her father she began a lifelong academic collaboration. She meticulously detailed daily Irish life; a valuable lodestone of references for later use in her novels. Maria mixed with the Anglo-Irish gentry, and her aunt, Margaret Ruxton of Blackcastle, supplied her with the novels of Anne Radcliffe and William Godwin and encouraged her ambition to write.

Edgeworth's first published work in 1795 was 'Letters for Literary Ladies'. That same year 'An Essay on the Noble Science of Self-Justification', written for a female audience, states that the fair sex is endowed with an art of self-justification and women should use their gifts to continually challenge the force and power of men, especially their husbands, with wit and intelligence.

In 1796 her first children's book, 'The Parent's Assistant', which included the much loved short story 'The Purple Jar' was published.

In 1798 her father married for the fourth and last time, this time to Frances Beaufort. Frances was a year younger than Maria and they quickly became close.

'Practical Education' (1798) is a progressive work on education that combines the ideas of Locke and Rousseau with scientific inquiry. Edgeworth believed that "learning should be a positive experience and that the discipline of education is more important during the formative years than the acquisition of knowledge." The ultimate goal of Edgeworth's system was to create an independent thinker who understands the consequences of his or her actions.

Her first novel, 'Castle Rackrent' (1800) was published anonymously without her father's knowledge. It was an immediate success and firmly established Maria's appeal to the public.

'Belinda' (1801), was her first full-length novel. It dealt with love, courtship, and marriage, and she examined these as conflicts within her "own personality and environment; conflicts between reason and feeling, restraint and individual freedom, and society and free spirit." Startingly, 'Belinda' also included a depiction of interracial marriage between an African servant and an English farm-girl. Later editions of the novel, in line with unforgiving times, removed these sections.

Frances also pushed the family to travel more first London (1800), the Midlands (1802) and later the continent; first to Brussels and then to France. They met all the notables, with Maria even receiving a proposal of marriage from a Swedish courtier.

'Tales of Fashionable Life' (1809 and 1812) is a 2-series collection of short stories that often had its focus on the life of women. The second series was so successful that she was now the most commercially successful novelist of her age and ranked alongside her contemporaries Jane Austen and Sir Walter Scott.

On a visit to London in 1813, she met many notables including Lord Byron. She entered into a long correspondence with Sir Walter Scott after the publication of 'Waverley' in 1814, in which he acknowledged her influence, and they formed a lasting friendship. She visited him in Scotland at Abbotsford House in 1823 and the following year he visited Edgeworthstown.

After debating the issue with the economist David Ricardo, Maria came to believe that better management and the further use of science in agriculture would raise food production and help to lower prices. They were both in favour of Catholic Emancipation, enfranchisement for Catholics without property restrictions, agricultural reform and increased educational opportunities for women.

She worked particularly hard to improve the living standards of the poor in Edgeworthstown and to provide schools for the local children whatever their denomination.

After her father's death in 1817 she edited his memoirs, and extended them with her biographical addenda. Her father had married 4 times and sired 22 children. At the height of her creative endeavours, Maria had written, "Seriously it was to please my Father I first exerted myself to write, to please him I continued."

Maria worked for the relief of the famine-stricken Irish peasants during the Irish Potato Famine. She wrote 'Orlandino' and gave the proceeds to the Relieve Fund. However, during the famine her 'business head' insisted that only those tenants who had paid their full rent would receive any relief. She also punished any tenants who voted against her Tory preferences.

'Helen' (1834) is Maria Edgeworth's final novel, the only one she wrote after her father's death. Here the focus was on characters and situation and not moral lessons.

William Rowan Hamilton was elected president of the Royal Irish Academy and Maria's advice was constantly sought especially regarding literature in Ireland. She suggested that women should be allowed to participate in Academy events. Hamilton made Maria an honorary member in 1837.

After a visit to see her relations Maria was struck with severe chest pains and died suddenly of a heart attack in Edgeworthstown on 22nd May 1849. She was 81.

Maria Edgeworth is buried in the family tomb at St. John's Church, Edgeworthstown, Longford, Ireland.


Maria Edgeworth – A Concise Bibliography

Letters for Literary Ladies (1795) Second Edition (1798)
An Essay on the Noble Science of Self-Justification (1795)
The Parent's Assistant (1796)
Practical Education (1798) (2 Vols; collaborated with her father and step-mother)
Castle Rackrent (1800) Novel
Early Lessons (1801)
Moral Tales (1801)
Belinda (1801) Novel
The Mental Thermometer (1801)

Essay on Irish Bulls (1802)
Popular Tales (1804)
The Modern Griselda (1804)
Moral Tales for Young People (1805) (6 Vols)
Leonora (1806)
Essays in Professional Education (1809)
Tales of Fashionable Life (1809)
Ennui (1809) Novel
The Absentee (1812) Novel
Patronage (1814) Novel
Harrington (1817) Novel
Ormond (1817) Novel
Comic Dramas (1817)
Memoirs of Richard Lovell Edgeworth (1820) Editor
Rosamond: A Sequel to Early Lessons (1821)
Frank: A Sequel to Frank in Early Lessons (1822)
Tomorrow (1823) Novel
Helen (1834) novel
Orlandino (1848) Temperance novel